BANKING LAW ESSENTIALS

KAROL K. SPARKS

AMERICAN BAR ASSOCIATION

Business Law Section

Cover design by Catherine Zaccarine.

Page layout by Quadrum Solutions.

The materials contained herein represent the opinions of the authors and/or the editors, and should not be construed to be the views or opinions of the law firms or companies with whom such persons are in partnership with, associated with, or employed by, nor of the American Bar Association or the Business Law Section unless adopted pursuant to the bylaws of the Association.

Nothing contained in this book is to be considered as the rendering of legal advice for specific cases, and readers are responsible for obtaining such advice from their own legal counsel. This book is intended for educational and informational purposes only.

Printed in the United States of America.

26 25 24 23 5 4 3 2

ISBN: 978-1-63905-075-8

Contents

Acknowledgements

I am indebted to so many people for the long career I have been privileged to enjoy: first, of course, my family—this was not always an easy ride for them; second, my firms, Barack Ferrazzano and before that Krieg DeVault—how lucky I was to find both of you at the right times in my life (or did you find me?); third, a whole host of wonderful clients who continuously challenged me; fourth, all my colleagues in the banking bar who encouraged and supported me; and fifth, the top-tier law schools who permitted me to teach their amazing students as we moved from place to place (Iowa, Wake Forest, Boston University). As my mother would say, I was "caught in a current of have to's" and you all helped me steer through the rapids.

Along the way, the greatest privilege was teaching Banking Law Basics and then Banking Law Fundamentals with lawyers/teachers who, regardless of their own challenges and "have to's," always answered the call. We started in 1998 and taught twice a year, except for Covid, and our core faculty included (in order of joining us):

Ted McAniff (yes, Ted and I started in 1998)
John Baerst*
Ed Lane-Reticker*
Jim Scott*
Bill Kroener
Sara Kelsey
Rosie Oda

Virgil Mattingly
John Buchman
Jeremy Newell
Camille Orme
High Conroy
Scott Alvarez
Helen Lee
John Geiringer

Some have retired. Some we have lost* and we miss them always.

It is a joy "when the band gets back together." Fingers crossed for 2022 and forward in Chicago and Boston.

Karol Sparks
Salem, South Carolina

1

Curbing the Anxiety

Welcome to My World

The first day I was tapped to be a banking law associate (as an insecure second year), the name partner who was the head of our banking practice group asked me to read the Bank Holding Company Act and Regulation Y in preparation for a client meeting. I did so. Within hours, I was summoned to his splendid corner office, introduced to the president of a community bank, and invited to sit at the large corner table. I immediately assumed the associate's position with pen in hand poised above the legal pad. But my role of notetaker was not to be. My boss turned to me and said (and I kid you not), "Karol, will you explain to Mr. [ ] why he should consider forming a bank holding company for his bank?" In total panic, I wracked my brain for anything . . . anything in response. Suffice it to say, after a thoroughly degrading minute, the first words I ever uttered to a bank client were "I don't know."

I tell that story for a couple of reasons.

First, it lets you know that all is not lost. If I could make it in this business with such a rocky beginning (and I actually successfully represented that same client for many years), there is hope.

Second, it helps explain my passion for teaching this complex area of law so that no one else suffers the same indignity.

And third, it reminds all of us that technical knowledge of the law is not practicing law—practicing law is turning that knowledge into advice.

I was clearly a "zero-basis" banking attorney and over the years I have taught many zero-basis law students and lawyers. While I disagree fundamentally with delivering the answers to the mysteries of banking law without the history and nuance, I recognize the need and decided to write this book.

Striving toward Simplification

We would not need this or any other book if banking law were navigable through self-study. It is an understatement to say that it is complicated on many, many levels. It is also an acronym-rich environment. And there is so much reading—it is difficult to know where to start. This book simplifies the process in four ways:

Oh, Those Acronyms and Obscure References

To navigate the acronyms, jargon, and obscure historical references to cases and statutes, please use the "Acronyms, Lingo, and Jargon" appendix at the end of this book and look up every reference you don't understand as you read (and in your practice). This is our lingo—understand it and use it.

Short Cites and Footnotes

This book would be full of short cites and too many footnotes if I treated each chapter as a stand-alone. So, ***terms are short cited in bold font the first time I use them*** and, ***to the extent possible, citations to applicable law are provided once.***

Table Presentation

If it works to display information in table format, that is how I present it. I find rows and columns very comforting, and I hope you do as well.

Tips

Watch for helpful tips and references to additional reading material presented in shaded box form (like that below) throughout this book.

Tips are presented in this format.

Getting Started on the Substance

There are a few nuggets about the business of banking that are essential for you to understand as soon as possible, beginning with perhaps the most essential question of all: What is a "bank"?; followed by how to know your client; and, finally, addressing our role as risk advisers.

What Is a "Bank"?

We throw the term "bank" around a lot, not as a term of law or art, but as a general describer of a type of entity that takes insured deposits from the public and reinvests them in the economy. The word thus encompasses a host of financial intermediaries that fund their operations through gathering cheap deposits—demand deposit accounts (a.k.a. transaction accounts, a.k.a. your checking account). They literally create money by taking in deposits payable on demand (you "demand" your money back when you write a check, use your debit card or transfer money out electronically) and lending the money longer term to customers and investing in high grade debt. Because they are susceptible to runs by depositors (who historically lined up as much as around the block), they are protected by a federal subsidy of deposit insurance.

All that means we should really be using the term "insured depository institution" or "**IDI**" when we talk about the law and the regulatory regime applicable to this type of intermediary. After all, IDIs are the focus of this book. However, Insured Depository Law lacks a certain cache and I draw the line at calling this book "Insured Depository Law Essentials." So, understand that when we say "bank," we may mean a variety of regulated entities that take deposits and have some laws in common, but, for the most part, have different regulatory regimes that apply.

Know Your Client

Our clients can be any one of a variety of IDI options. We cannot get past Chapter 1 without going through the "name that charter" process.

Charter Choices. We call the different kinds of IDIs "charters," meaning the form of organization of the entity. Simplistically, we have:

Commercial banks: are characterized historically as those intermediaries that combine business banking with consumer banking. They have the word "bank" in their legal names. Under applicable law, no other type of entity (except some bank affiliates) may use the word "bank" in their name generally without regulatory approval.

Savings associations or savings and loan associations: were created primarily to take savings deposits from individuals and make 1-4 family mortgage loans. Their charter limits the amount of business loans they can make. They usually have the word "savings" in their legal names but beware they may use "savings bank," even though they are not commercial banks.

Credit unions: were created as not-for-profit, member-owned entities to take deposits from individuals and make short-term unsecured personal loans, with all customers being members with a common bond (employer groups, associations, communities, etc.). They have "credit union" in their name.

Others: some states have spawned a variety of similar species, predominate of which are industrial loan companies. They are generally owned by nonbanking companies and are limited by federal law regarding their ability to take demand deposits and make commercial loans—they must choose one or the other.

The Dual Banking System. But, there is more—each charter comes in flavors. Unique to the United States (and a creature of legislative accident), we have a "**dual banking system**." That means, we have federal charters, literally IDIs organized under the laws of the United States, and we have state charters, IDIs formed under the laws of the several states, commonwealths, and territories. The dual banking system exists for commercial banks, savings associations, and credit unions. They are distinguished from each other by naming conventions that require:

Federal Charter	Naming Requirement
Federally chartered commercial banks	Must have "National" or "NA" (for National Association) in the legal name
Federally chartered savings association and savings banks	Must have "Federal" or "FSA" (for Federal Savings Association) or "FSB" (for Federal Savings Bank") in the legal name
Federally chartered credit unions	Must have "Federal Credit Union" or "FCU" in the legal name

State banks frequently use "Bank & Trust Company" in their names, but only if they have trust/fiduciary powers, and, frankly, there is no general rule.

A degree of confusion arises because any of these institutions may market themselves using abbreviated names and logos, so you may not be able to tell the charter type from the signage or advertising materials. What is Citi? What is Wells Fargo? What is Truist?

> *Best to check the FDIC's Bank Find website and look up your client to verify the type of charter.*
>
> *https://banks.data.fdic.gov/bankfind-suite/bankfind*

It Is a Risky Business. . . and We Are Risk Advisers

Banks fund with cheap, no interest, or very low interest-earning deposits. Think about it. They borrow your money and pay virtually nothing to you. Then they expend it primarily on other financial assets that may or may not prove profitable. A very risky business—on an industry-wide basis and on a bank-by-bank basis.

During the past decade, the bank regulatory agencies have increasingly emphasized the importance of sound risk management processes and strong internal controls when evaluating the activities of the IDIs they supervise. Properly managing risk has been identified as critical to the conduct of safe and sound banking activities and has become even more important as new technologies, product innovation, and the size and speed of financial transactions have changed the nature of banking markets. The agencies have identified a spectrum of risks facing a banking institution including, but not limited to, *credit, market, liquidity, operational, legal,* and *reputational risk.*

As lawyers, we have become risk advisors. We used to evaluate legality and give our clients the proverbial green, yellow, or red light. Today that is just the starting point—we give a green light legally and then we have to identify and discuss the risks associated with that activity or investment and make sure our clients have the infrastructure to identify, measure, and monitor that risk. Think about an IDI taking deposits from a payment processor or a check cashier or partnering with fintechs; investing in complicated derivatives; permitting customers to invest in cryptocurrencies; entering into a new line of business; paying incentive compensation. . . .What are the risks? How can they be mitigated and managed?

History Is Crucial (but Can Wait)

In the words of John D. Hawke, Jr., Comptroller of the Currency from 1998–2004, "Students of probability theory tell us that if enough monkeys pounded away for a sufficiently long time, they will eventually reproduce the entire works of Shakespeare. It seems unlikely, however, that even those intrepid monkeys could recreate our present system of financial regulation."[1] While a gross exaggeration (monkeys crafting Shakespeare??), Mr. Hawke makes an excellent point that the U.S. system of financial regulation is not rational, and it is unlike anything else in the world.

What you have to understand in this regard is that no one took out a whiteboard and started drawing boxes and arrows horizontally and then more boxes and arrows vertically and, *voila*, created this system. On the contrary, Congress's actions in crafting banking laws have been reactive, oftentimes to crisis and sometimes to innovation, and the result is improvisational. As a result, to ultimately understand this complex area of law, we must dig into our history and figure out the myriad answers to one simple question: WHY?

The day I learned the history is the day I really understood what I was doing. That said, my premise in writing this book, and the promise I want from readers, is that you will digest this basic, essential information, stop hyperventilating, and, finally, thirst for an understanding of "why" our banking system is this complicated. For that deep dive, I offer *Keys to Banking Law,* now in its third edition.

1. Legal Times, June 13, 1983, at 34.

2

Regulatory Rudiments

Regulation, Supervision, and Enforcement

Federal and state banking laws impose a comprehensive system of regulation, supervision, and enforcement on the operations of IDIs that is intended primarily for the protection of the insured deposits and depositors of banks. This framework is enforced by bank regulatory agencies at both the federal and state level. In this regard:

Regulation	Means that the federal or state agency has rulemaking authority under the applicable statute and the authority to interpret the law, typically with some degree of judicial deference.
Supervision	Means examination authority and licensing authority (the ability to require applications, notices, and registrations).
Enforcement	Means the ability of the agency to enforce safety and soundness and compliance with laws.

If we drill down a little deeper, regulation is the basic topic of this book—our search for the law and how to apply it. But we also need to be keenly aware of the other elements.

On the supervisory front, depository institutions are subject to regular examinations by their respective regulatory agencies, which result in examination reports and ratings that are not publicly available and can impact the conduct and growth of business. These examinations consider not only compliance with applicable laws and regulations, but also capital levels, asset quality and risk, management ability and performance, earnings, liquidity, and various other factors.

On the enforcement front, the regulatory agencies generally have broad discretion to impose restrictions and limitations on the operations of a regulated entity where the agencies determine, among other things, that such operations are unsafe or unsound, fail to comply with applicable law, or are otherwise inconsistent with laws and regulations. They can also bring action against persons involved in banking (and that can include lawyers).

The Bank Regulators

Our legal framework is disparate when we view the bank regulatory agencies in regard to regulation, supervision, and enforcement. One agency may be responsible for a bank charter across the board; others have split responsibility; and still others have targeted responsibility. To this end, the regulatory agencies fall into categories as to whether they are the "chartering authority" and/or the "primary federal regulator" or have a secondary or targeted role in the supervision of depository institutions.

Chartering Authorities

To form a depository institution, the organizers will approach the chartering authority. Because institutions may be federal or state chartered, there are chartering authorities at each level.

National Banks and Federal Savings Associations	**Comptroller of the Currency** The first federal banking agency created by Congress in the National Bank Act after the Civil War was the Office of the Comptroller of the Currency (**OCC** or the **Comptroller**). The OCC was structured as an office in the Treasury Department to charter and supervise what was then a new kind of bank, national banks, and to regulate the distribution of currency these banks were authorized to issue (hence the name "Comptroller *of the Currency*"). The OCC was to write uniform rules that would apply to all national banks and send examiners into the banks to make sure those rules were being followed. Following the Global Financial Crisis of 2008–2009, Congress also conferred the chartering authority of federal savings associations on the OCC.

Federal Credit Unions	**National Credit Union Administration** The National Credit Union Administration (**NCUA**) is the chartering authority for federal credit unions. It was created by Congress in 1970 to replace earlier regulators. It is an independent federal agency.
State Banks, Savings Associations, and Credit Unions	**State Departments of Financial Institutions** The respective state departments of financial institutions are chartering authorities for state banks, state savings associations, and state credit unions. Several states also charter other types of depository institutions, like industrial loan companies.

Primary Federal Regulators

As indicated above, bank regulatory agencies do far more than charter institutions. For this reason, Congress recognized a need for federal agencies to have the primary authority to examine and supervise insured banks and savings associations. These agencies are referred to in many publications, and in this book, as "primary federal regulators." Responsibilities of the primary federal regulator include:

- conducting examinations;
- initiating supervisory and enforcement actions;
- assigning composite examination ratings;
- approving branch and other applications;
- reviewing change of control applications; and
- approving mergers (if it is the primary federal regulator of the resulting institution).

The OCC is both chartering authority and primary federal regulator for national banks and federal savings associations. Likewise, the NCUA serves in both capacities for federal credit unions.

Here is the rub: Congress decided that state institutions needed a federal watchdog—that state departments of financial institutions could not stand alone as the supervisor of state charters. Accordingly, Congress looked to two existing federal agencies to serve as the primary federal regulators of state banks: the Federal Deposit Insurance Corporation (**FDIC**) and the Board of Governors of the Federal Reserve System (**Federal Reserve**).

State banks may choose to join the Federal Reserve System (by purchasing stock of the local Federal Reserve Bank) and thereby have the

Federal Reserve as the primary federal regulatory agency. They are known as "**state member banks.**" Or, if they did not choose such membership, they have the FDIC as the primary federal regulatory agency and are known as "**state nonmember banks.**"

State savings associations have the FDIC as their primary federal regulator. State credit unions have the NCUA.

Secondary Regulators

This term is not defined in federal law. It has been used in several charts published by regulatory agencies to distinguish the authority that the agencies exercise as primary federal regulators and the authority that the FDIC and Federal Reserve exercise in their respective capacities as insurers of deposits and all things monetary.

The FDIC. The FDIC administers the deposit insurance fund (**DIF**) under the Federal Deposit Insurance Act for the benefit of depositors of banks and savings associations, with the objective that insured depositors are protected from loss without recourse to taxpayer funding. It assesses banks for the cost of FDIC insurance and serves as receiver for failed bank assets.

The Federal Reserve. The Federal Reserve is actually a system, organized under the Federal Reserve Act with the Board of Governors (**Board**) in Washington, D.C., and 12 Federal Reserve Banks scattered across the country. It wears many hats. In addition to being a primary federal regulator, as discussed above, it: regulates bank and thrift holding companies and systemically important financial institutions; facilitates our payments system; and has rulemaking authority under numerous federal laws. It is also our central bank and lender of last resort to the financial markets through its discount window operations, both of which have become part of its implementation of the monetary policy of the United States.

Targeted Regulators

Congress also bestows other lines of targeted authority within these agencies (the FDIC, for example, has authority to approve certain activities of state banks and their subsidiaries), but there are also nonbanking agencies that have rulemaking authority affecting depository institutions.

FinCEN. For instance, offices in the Treasury Department, such as the Financial Crimes Enforcement Network (**FinCEN**), enforce money laundering and currency transactions regulations.

CFPB. Further, among the "targeted regulators" is the Bureau of Consumer Financial Protection (yes, "Bureau" is the first word in the name in the statute, but the acronym adopted by the agency is **CFPB**). It has power over all consumer financial products and services and is funded right out of the Federal Reserve's budget. The CFPB began operations July

21, 2011, at which time it succeeded to all regulatory authority to prescribe rules or issue orders or guidelines (the so called "consumer financial protection functions") transferred from the Federal Reserve, OCC, FDIC, FTC (with some limits) and HUD (the U.S. Department of Housing and Urban Development). The CFPB has rulemaking authority under a wide spectrum of federal consumer protection laws and examination authority over IDIs of $10 billion in assets and larger.

The Bank Regulators' Universe

All of this boils down to the following as to IDIs:

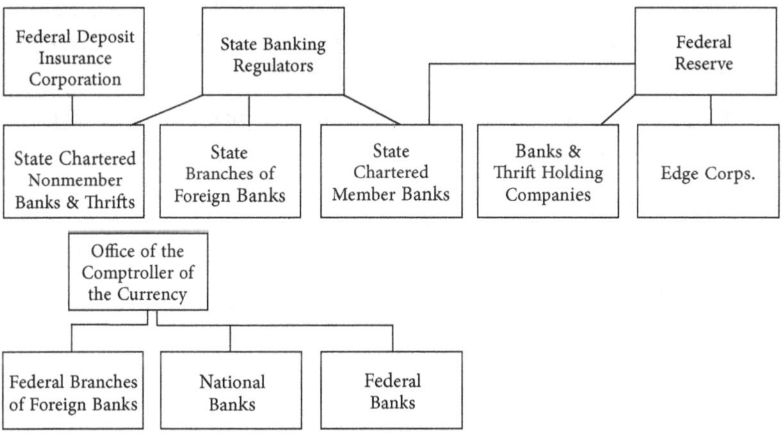

How many banks and thrifts does each regulator oversee? The chart below illustrates the distribution of deposits and offices by charter class as of June 30, 2020.

> *The FDIC provides bank data and statistics on insured institutions at https://www7.fdic.gov/sod/sodSummary.asp?barItem=3.*

National Totals—by Charter Class as of June 30, 2020

Charter Class	Number of Institutions	Number of Offices	Deposits ($000) for June 30, 2020
Commercial Banks	4,430	79,416	14,490,500,234
National Charter	779	39,707	9,615,139,353
State Charter	3,651	39,709	4,875,360,881
Federal Reserve Member	702	12,720	2,179,209,868
Federal Reserve Nonmember	2,949	26,989	2,696,151,013
Savings Institutions	636	5,624	1,054,195,383
Federal Charter Savings Associations	285	2,176	447,454,814
State Charter Savings Institutions	351	3,448	606,740,569
FDIC-Supervised Savings Banks	315	3,143	291,369,403
Federal Reserve-Supervised	36	305	315,371,166

Based on information reported by credit unions to the NCUA, as of September 30, 2020, there were 5,133 federally insured credit unions with 123.7 million members. Total assets in federally insured credit unions was $1.79 trillion.

Finding the Law

Given that our clients may have a variety of charters and may have any number of affiliates, we must know where to find the applicable law. Banking law moves from the statutes to the regulations promulgated by the agency with rulemaking authority, to the abundant sources of less formal guidance in the form of interpretive letters, application approvals, depository institution letters and notices, and various types of handbooks.

The following outlines federal banking law—remember there are schemes in each state, commonwealth, and territory as well.

Statutes

Rule number one: most of our federal statutes are codified in Title 12 of the U.S. Code (**U.S.C.**). They are codified in the order of enactment. It sounds easy, but what complicates the process is that most of the laws and all of the modern laws, are "amending" statutes, meaning you cannot simply open 12 U.S.C. and find them. You find bits and pieces strewn throughout. To read the actual act, you must locate the conference report and work your way through it. As can be seen below, only the laws in italics have a formal place in the code.

National Bank Act 1864 (**NBA**)	**12 U.S.C. § 1**
Federal Reserve Act of 1913 (**FRA**)	**12 U.S.C. § 241**
Home Owners' Loan Act (**HOLA**)	**12 U.S.C. § 1462**
Federal Credit Union Act (**FCUA**)	**12 U.S.C. § 1752**
Glass-Steagall Act of 1933	
Federal Deposit Insurance Act 1935, 1950 (**FDIA**)	**12 U.S.C. § 1811**
Bank Holding Company Act of 1956, 1970 (**BHCA**)	**12 U.S.C. § 1841**
*Savings and Loan Holding Company Act of 1959 (***S&LHCA***)*	**12 U.S.C. § 1467**
International Banking Act of 1978	**12 U.S.C. § 1878**

Depository Institutions Deregulation and Monetary Control Act of 1980

Garn-St Germain Act 1982

Money Laundering Control Act of 1986

Competitive Equality Banking Act of 1987

Financial Institutions Reform, Recovery and Enforcement Act of 1989 (**FIRREA**)

Federal Deposit Insurance Corporation Improvement Act of 1991 (**FDICIA**)

Riegle-Neal Interstate Banking and Branching Efficiency Act of 1994 (**Riegle-Neal**)

Gramm-Leach-Bliley Act of 1999 (**Gramm-Leach-Bliley**)

Emergency Economic Stabilization Act of 2008

Dodd-Frank Wall Street Reform and Consumer Protection Act of 2010 (**Dodd-Frank**)

Economic Growth, Regulatory Relief, and Consumer Protection Act of 2018 (**Regulatory Relief Act**)

The laws discussed in this book are short cited above and the citations to U.S.C. (where applicable) are provided as well. Mark this page for quick reference.

Regulations

Regulations are formal rulemakings promulgated under federal statutes and are subject to the rigors of public comment under the Administrative Procedures Act. Notices of Proposed Rulemaking (**NPR**) and Final Rules are published in the Federal Register.

Rule number two: the regulations are then codified in Title 12 of the Code of Federal Regulations (**C.F.R.**). They are also in order from the first agency created to the last. Thus, the OCC holds pole position, followed by the Federal Reserve, the FDIC, the NCUA, and the newest kid on the block, the CFPB.

12 C.F.R. 1–199	Comptroller of the Currency
12 C.F.R. 200's	Federal Reserve System (Conveniently identified by letter of the alphabet, the order of which coincides with the part of the C.F.R. Thus, Regulation D—the fourth letter of the alphabet—is 12 C.F.R. 204.) The Federal Reserve's bank regulations for member banks are in Regulation H -12 CFR Part 208.
12 C.F.R. 300's	Federal Deposit Insurance Corporation
12 C.F.R. 700's	National Credit Union Administration
12 C.F.R. 1000's	Bureau of Consumer Financial Protection (Using the same letter system as the Federal Reserve. Thus, Regulation E—the fifth letter of the alphabet—is 12 C.F.R. 1005.)

Savings Association regulations:

12 C.F.R. 100's	OCC – Federal Thrifts (Many of these have been removed and regulations applicable previously to national banks are now allocable to both.)
12 C.F.R. 390/391	FDIC – State thrifts
12 C.F.R. 238/239	Federal Reserve – Thrift holding companies (Reg LL) and mutual holding companies (Reg MM)

Who issues what regulations? The answer starts simple and then, like everything in banking law, gets complicated.

Simple	Rulemaking Authority
Chartering Authority	All regulations under the empowering act—the OCC under the NBA and HOLA; the NCUA under the FCUA; state banking regulators under applicable state law. That includes rules on charter requirements and steps to obtain a charter, powers and investments, applications and licensing, branching and nonbranch offices, lending limits. . .
Primary Federal Regulator	Usually, they each issue similar or virtually identical regulations to address supervision—examples include: capital, safety and soundness, privacy, management official interlocks, community reinvestment, sales of insurance. . . That is why many footnotes in this book include citations to all three sets of regulations—OCC, FDIC and the Federal Reserve. (See fn. 2 as an example.)
CFPB	All consumer protection laws assigned to the CFPB by Dodd-Frank and unfair, deceptive, and abusive trade practices.
More Complicated	**Rulemaking Authority**
Federal Reserve	Generally, all regulations under the FRA, BHCA, and S&LHCA, including those regarding: member banks (Regulation H); international banking (Regulation K); affiliate transactions under Sections 23A and B (Regulation W); reserves and kinds of deposits (Regulation D); the BHCA (Regulation Y) and S&LHCA (Regulations LL and MM); funds availability and collection of checks (Regulation CC); Unlawful Internet Gambling (Regulation GG); permitted broker-dealer activities of banks (Regulation R); interchange fees (Regulation II); enhanced prudential standards (Regulation YY); and anything having to do with payments, monetary control, and the discount window. *It is actually easier to read the Table of Contents of the 12 C.F.R 200's. The Federal Reserve wears lots of hats.*

FDIC	Regulations under the FDIA, including those regarding: deposit insurance coverage and assessments and brokered deposit rules (Part 330); advertising FDIC insurance (Part 328); failed IDIs and receiverships; and principal activities of insured state banks and savings associations (Part 362).

Interpretations, Guidelines, Bulletins, and Other Resources

Thankfully, the internet creates a convenient drop zone for our less formal law:

www.occ.treas.gov

www.federalreserve.gov

www.fdic.gov

www.ncua.gov

www.consumerfinance.gov

A Note on Guidance and other Sources of "Law"

Each one of the websites listed above is a treasure trove of supervisory guidance, interagency statements, bulletins, policy statements, examination manuals and checklists, speeches of import, decisions on cases and applications, and **FAQs** (frequently asked questions). The amount of information is overwhelming, and it has been historically difficult to parse the line between what is enforceable and what is really merely guidance.

More problematic, examiners were increasingly prone to treat supervisory guidance as law, noncompliance with which would be subject to **MRAs** (matters requiring attention), **MRIAs** (matters requiring immediate attention), and sometimes to regulatory enforcement actions. **But guidance is not law.** Finally, all of the bank regulatory agencies (yes, even the CFPB) realized the necessity of transparency in this regard and, in 2018, collectively issued what they like to call "guidance on guidance"—officially entitled, "The Interagency Statement Clarifying the Role of Supervisory Guidance."[1] The FDIC, CFPB, and NCUA then codified this guidance in individual regulations.[2] The agencies clarified that "unlike a law or regulation, supervisory guidance does not have the force and effect of law, and the agencies do not take enforcement actions based on supervisory guidance.

1. The Federal Reserve issued the interagency Statement as SR 18-5 / CA 18-7 (September 12, 2018).
2. (FDIC) 12 C.F.R. Part 302; (CFPB) 12 C.F.R. Part 1074; (NCUA) 12 C.F.R. Part 791.

Rather, supervisory guidance outlines the agencies' supervisory expectations or priorities and articulates the agencies' general views regarding appropriate practices for a given subject area."

The problem remains—determining what is law and what is guidance can be nuanced.

A Note on Administrative Law and Deference

When banking issues reach the courts, whether it be on the appropriateness of an approval of an application, or an enforcement against a bank or affiliated party, or in connection with rulemaking or whatever final agency action is ripe for review, the scope of review by the courts is generally under the Administrative Procedures Act[3] and the standard to set aside agency action is oftentimes "arbitrary, capricious, an abuse of discretion or otherwise not in accordance with law."

When final federal agency action is under the judicial microscope, the courts are bound to give the banking agency "deference," if deserving. Our banking law is rife with examples of significant cases where deference has been the deciding factor, especially in the arena of new powers.

In this regard, the seminal *Chevron*[4] doctrine of administrative deference has a two-part test established by the Supreme Court for reviewing the construction of a statute by a regulatory agency charged with the duty to administer the statute. To this end, the court must first determine whether "Congress has directly spoken to the precise question at issue. If the intent of Congress is clear, this is the end of the matter; for the court, as well as the agency, must give effect to the unambiguously expressed intent of Congress." If, however, the court determines that Congress has not directly addressed the precise question, the court may not simply impose its own construction on the statute: "Rather, if the statute is silent or ambiguous, with respect to the specific issue, the question for the court is whether the agency's answer is based on a permissible construction of the statute. A court may not substitute its own construction of a statutory provision for a reasonable interpretation made by the administrator of an agency."[5]

That last sentence is powerful stuff, precluding a court's *de novo* construction of the law. There are so many examples of this application, but no more than when the OCC was pushing the envelope on national bank powers. For example, in an early case applying the *Chevron* doctrine to a decision of the OCC regarding the insurance powers of national banks, the D.C. Circuit Court reasoned:

---

3. 5 U.S.C. § 706.
4. Chevron USA v. Natural Resources Defense Council, 467 U.S. 837 (1984) ("*Chevron*").
5. 467 U.S. 837, 842-845.

> To overturn the Comptroller's construction, we would have to conclude that it is "so inconsistent" with a "sufficiently clear" statutory policy as to demonstrate that "Congress's clear intent has been violated."[6]

6. Independent Ins. Agents of Am. v. Ludwig, 997 F.2d at 961 (citing Investment Co. Inst. v. Conover, 790 F.2d 925, 935 (D.C. Cir. 1986)). *See also,* NationsBank of North Carolina, N.A. v. Variable Annuity Life Ins. Co., 513 U.S. 251 (1995) regarding annuity sales.

3

"Bank" Charters

The Dual Banking System

We have national banks and state banks; we have federal savings associations and state savings associations; and we have federal and state credit unions. That is our "**dual banking**" system. Understand: it was a mistake, not a carefully crafted plan. It has survived many a crisis and numerous calls for "rationalization." Yet, the system still lies at the heart of American banking. In some respects, it reflects the best of our founding fathers, Alexander Hamilton and Thomas Jefferson: large national banking institutions imbued with the right to preempt state laws that significantly interfere with their operations (*a la* Hamilton's vision) versus state-chartered, community-focused banks and savings and loans (*a la* Jefferson's vision). That does not mean all big banks and thrifts are federally chartered and all small banks and thrifts are state chartered, but, as time goes by, it is getting closer to being true.

Charter Choices

You were introduced to these charters in Chapter 1, but each has its own characteristics.

National Banks

A national bank is merely a commercial bank, the organizers of which elect regulation under federal law. The laws that apply to national banks are crafted by the Congress of the United States and are codified primarily in the NBA in Title 12 of the U.S.C., beginning with 12 U.S.C. section 1. The OCC, a bureau of the Department of Treasury, regulates national banks. The Comptroller of the Currency is actually a person appointed by Congress, and when the OCC is sued, the Comptroller gets sued in his own name. Much of the "law" with respect to national bank activities is found in OCC interpretive letters, approvals of applications, supervisory letters, and regulatory guidance. This treasure trove of informal law is now available on the Comptroller's website: www.occ.treas.gov.

National banks must comply with a complex web of laws and regulations. This includes not only supervision and regulation by the Comptroller, but also by the Federal Reserve System, because national banks are required to be members of the Federal Reserve, and also the FDIC, because the deposits of national banks are FDIC insured.

The activities of national banks are highly regulated under 12 U.S.C. Section 24 (Seventh), which limits bank powers to the "business of banking" and activities "incident thereto," and, in some respects, the powers are different from those of state banks; so too are the locations at which they do business. In this regard, certain core banking activities—lending money, taking deposits, and cashing checks—may be conducted solely at legally established branches.

What particularly distinguishes national banks from their state bank brethren is that they enjoy enormous benefit from preemption of state laws. As a consequence, most of the largest banks in the nation flocked to national bank charters in the 1980s and 1990s as the OCC pushed the preemption envelope further and further.

State Banks

A state bank is a commercial bank organized under the laws of a particular state. Each of the fifty states and commonwealths, the District of Columbia, and the U.S. territories charter banks under the authority of state law. In some states, banks begin life as corporations and then are granted bank charters; in other states, bank charters are special and not subject to corporate law. Sometimes bank corporate documents may be filed with the appropriate secretary of state; sometimes only the state regulator can make those filings; and sometimes nothing may be filed there. Sometimes state banks must qualify to do business in other states, like corporations, but mostly not. Sometimes they must register with the foreign bank regulator as a foreign bank (especially if they have an office in the state). Sometimes, not. Yes, it is terribly confusing. One fact that is just about universally true: generally, a state bank will need written permission from the foreign state bank regulator to use its bank name in a state in which it is entering.

Notwithstanding state chartering authority, state banks are subject to federal supervision and regulation by either the FDIC or the Federal Reserve.

Nonmember Banks	Unless they voluntarily become members of the Federal Reserve, state banks are "nonmember banks" and are supervised and regulated by the FDIC.
Member Banks	If a state bank chooses to join the Federal Reserve (which it does by buying the stock of the Federal Reserve Bank in its district), it is characterized as a "member bank" with supervision and regulation by the Federal Reserve. *The Federal Reserve deposits most of the regulations applicable to member banks in one place: 12 C.F.R. Part 208.*

The federal regulators do not determine bank powers. Each state legislature generally determines the powers of the banks organized domestically. While the statutory schemes are somewhat disparate from state to state, the powers of banks are generally confined to those that are closely related to banking. The authority for state banks to engage in activities derives from three types of statutory sources: express statutory authorization; incidental powers determined by the state regulator; and so-called "wild card" or parity provisions, which permit state banks to exercise any power permitted to national banks or other financial institutions.

That said, states may not go too far in authorizing state banks to engage in risky activities—under federal law, they may not engage as principal in any activity not permissible for a national bank, unless the FDIC determines that the activity would not pose a significant risk to the federal deposit insurance funds and the state bank is in compliance with federal capital requirements.[1]

Federal Savings Associations

Federal savings associations, including federal savings banks, are financial institutions organized under the HOLA. They are frequently referred to as "**thrifts**." They were originally organized in mutual form, meaning they were owned by their depositors (many converted to stock form in later years). The charter was conceived in order to stimulate savings by consumers and to provide funds for retail mortgages. Although the law still provides that such associations are organized, in part, to provide "for the extension of credit for homes and other goods and services,"[2] in recent decades, their banking powers have veered more closely to those of national banks.

1. FDCIA, 12 U.S.C. § 1831a(a).
2. 12 U.S.C. § 1464(a).

Federal associations had been supervised and regulated by the Office of Thrift Supervision (**OTS**), formerly an office of the U.S. Treasury Department,[3] since its predecessor, the Federal Home Loan Bank Board was abolished by Congress in 1989.[4] The OTS was eliminated on July 21, 2011, through a merger with the OCC by virtue of the Dodd-Frank Act. The OTS's supervisory responsibilities with respect to federal savings associations were allocated to the OCC. The deposits of federal associations are insured by the FDIC, by virtue of which the FDIC obtains certain supervisory authority over federal thrifts.

One unique aspect of the federal thrift charter continues—it is required under HOLA to be and remain a "qualified thrift lender"[5] in order to preserve its original focus on mortgage lending. A **QTL** is a savings association that qualifies as a domestic building and loan association under Section 7701(a)(19) of the Internal Revenue Code or that has at least 65% of its portfolio assets in "qualified thrift investments." Investments that are considered "qualified thrift investments" include, among other things, loans and investments relating to domestic residential real estate or manufactured housing and mortgage-backed securities relating to the same, home equity loans, small business loans, educational loans, loans made through credit cards or credit card accounts, and shares of stock issued by any Federal Home Loan Bank, without limitation; and shares of stock issued by the Federal Home Loan Mortgage Corporation or the Federal National Mortgage Association, and 50% of the dollar amount of residential mortgage loans originated by the association and sold within 90 days, the aggregate of which is subject to a 20% of portfolio assets limitation.[6]

The OCC cuts the corner on national bank and federal thrift powers with its list of ***Activities Permissible for National Banks and Federal Savings Associations, Cumulative,*** *available for PDF download at*

www. OCC.treas.gov.

12 C.F.R. 7.1000 also includes lists of activities.

State Savings Associations

Savings associations may also be chartered by the several states in mutual or stock form. The states use a variety of names for this charter, including

3. 12 U.S.C. § 1462a.
4. Pub. L. No. 101-73, 103 Stat. 183, Title III.
5. 12 U.S.C. § 1467a(c)(3).
6. 12 U.S.C. § 1467a(m)(4)(c); 12 U.S.C. § 1464(c)(1).

building and loan associations, cooperative banks, and the like. These institutions, like federal associations, were created to facilitate the availability of credit for housing. Several states also charter savings banks under statutory schemes separate from those governing state savings associations.

The OTS had operated as the primary federal regulator of state associations until, as discussed above, the Dodd-Frank Act eliminated the agency. The transfer included all functions of the OTS related to state savings associations in the same manner with respect to the FDIC as described above regarding the OCC with federal associations.

The activities of state-chartered savings associations are determined in the first instance by the state chartering authority. In a parallel scheme to what was effected by Congress regarding state bank powers, a state savings association may not engage as principal in any activity not permissible for a federal savings association, unless the FDIC determines that the activity would not pose a significant risk to the federal deposit insurance fund and the savings association is in compliance with federal capital requirements.[7]

Industrial Loan Companies

ILCs are state-chartered institutions that originated in the early 1900s as finance companies for lower-income borrowers. These early ILCs offered relatively high-interest unsecured loans to factory workers who could not otherwise obtain credit.

ILCs are currently only chartered by California, Hawaii, Minnesota, Nevada, and Utah. But, it is really all about Utah, which became a favorite "nonbank bank" charterer for commercial companies that did not want to be regulated as bank holding companies. Under the BHCA, as discussed in Chapter 4, they have to trim their core activities—either take demand deposits or make commercial loans, but not both, in order for the parent company not to be regulated as a bank holding company. Most of the modern law regarding ILCs derives from the commercial companies that sought to enter banking through the ILC loophole.

FDIA Definitions

The definitions of depository institutions in Section 3 of the FDIA may be summarized as follows:

7. 12 U.S.C. § 1831e(a).

Banks

National Banks	Banks chartered by the OCC.
State Banks	State-chartered banks, which include trust companies, savings banks, industrial banks (or similar institutions that the FDIC finds to be operating in the same manner as an industrial bank), or other banking institutions that are "engaged in the business of receiving deposits, other than trust funds," and any cooperative bank or other unincorporated bank the deposits of which were insured by the FDIC on August 8, 1989 (the day before FIRREA was enacted).

Savings Associations

Federal Associations	Insured institutions with a federal savings association or federal savings bank charter which is chartered under 12 U.S.C. Section 1464 (granted by the OCC or the former OTS/Federal Home Loan Bank Board).
State Associations	Any building and loan association, savings and loan association, or homestead association; or any cooperative bank (other than a cooperative bank that is a state bank) that is organized and operating according to the laws of the state in which it is chartered or organized.

FDIC Deposit Insurance

The deposits of all of the above charters are insured by the FDIC in its capacity as administrator of the DIF for the benefit of depositors with the objective that insured depositors are protected from loss without recourse to taxpayer funding. The FDIC is tasked with maintaining the DIF so that adequate funds are available to protect insured depositors in the event of an institution's failure.

Deposits that are guaranteed to be insured are those within the **SMDIA**: the "standard maximum deposit insurance amount." With some complexity, it is now $250,000 per account ownership held in a given bank or savings association.[8]

8. The SMDIA is set under 12 U.S.C. § 1821(a)(B), as implemented by 12 C.F.R. Part 330.

Special Purpose Bank Charters

There are a variety of charters issued by the bank regulatory agencies that are banks, except for one reason or another they are not "banks." Some of these charters were historically denominated as "nonbank banks" and their purpose was primarily to avoid bank holding company status for the parent company.

The chartering authority of the OCC and the states includes the authority to charter special purpose banks. These banks may offer only a small number of products, target a limited customer base, incorporate nontraditional elements, or have narrowly targeted business plans. They are primarily trust banks, credit card banks, community development banks and bankers' banks. The organizers seek bank charters so they may exercise powers or extend consumer credit with the benefit of interest rate exportation (discussed below), but they do not intend to accept deposits (except that state trust companies have historically been required to hold one deposit account and be FDIC insured). Some prudential regulation applies to them. Some does not. Anti-money laundering laws and the Community Reinvestment Act typically do. You have to parse the statutes to figure it out on an entity-by-entity basis and review the approval documents for the specific charter, because the regulator may customize the charter and make approval conditional on compliance with certain laws.

The OCC devotes a portion of its Charters Booklet of the Comptroller's Licensing Manual to Special Purpose Proposals starting at page 50. See, https://www.occ.gov/publications/publications-by-type/licensing-manuals/charters.pdf.

Credit Unions

Federal Credit Unions

Like national banks and federal savings associations, federal credit unions are creatures of federal law. But, quite controversially, they are non-profit organizations and tax exempt. Unlike other "banks," they are owned by their members—depositors and borrowers—who are tied to a "common bond." Examples include: Military, Teachers, Company, and Residency. Thus, they do not issue stock and they build capital through retained earnings.

Credit union deposits are called share accounts. The NCUA protects the safety and soundness of the credit union system by identifying, monitoring, and reducing risks to the National Credit Union Share Insurance Fund (**NCUSIF**). Backed by the full faith and credit of the United States, the Share Insurance Fund provides up to $250,000 of federal share insurance to millions of account holders in all federal credit unions and the overwhelming majority of state-chartered credit unions.

State Credit Unions

Like state banks, credit unions may be organized under state law, except for Wyoming, Delaware, and South Dakota, which require federal incorporation. They are also member owned and tax exempt.

Commonalities and Differences in the Bank Charters

So, at the end of the day, how are national and state banks alike and different?

Commonalities

First, what they have in common. They all are subject to the regulatory, supervisory, and enforcement schemes described in this book; they all have deposit insurance; they all must comply with prudential regulation (as discussed in Chapter 6); they all are subject to rulemaking by the CFPB; they all must hold capital in accordance with applicable capital guidelines and maintain liquidity. Noteworthy are the following other commonalities:

Geographic Limits	Long gone are the days when banks were fenced in by their county or state lines. All depository institutions may open branch offices or merge with banks in their home state. "Well-capitalized" and "well-managed"[9] banks may establish new interstate branches or acquire individual branches of a bank in another state without impediments. They also may merge across state lines with approval of the primary federal regulatory agency with jurisdiction over the surviving bank.
Interest-rate Exportation	All depository institutions may export interest rates from their home office or branch locations, permitting them to avoid state usury laws under Section 85 of the NBA for national banks and Section 27 of the FDIA for state banks.

9. You will see these terms used frequently in this book. They are defined in Chapters 6 and 8, respectively.

Community Reinvestment	They all must meet the convenience and needs of their community under the Community Reinvestment Act (**CRA**). They are examined for compliance periodically by the federal agencies that are responsible for supervising the depository institution. The regime rewards (and punishes) through the application approval process, such that, in connection with every application for:[10] • a charter for a national bank or federal thrift; • deposit insurance for a newly chartered bank; • establishment of a branch; • relocation of a main office or branch; • a merger, consolidation, or deposit assumption under the Bank Merger Act; and • a BHC acquisition of shares of a regulated financial institution under Section 3 of the BHCA, the responsible agency must assess the applicant's, or each party's, history of meeting the convenience and needs of the community, and to that end, it must review the CRA record of the applicant and, if relevant, the target. But there is more. Notice of all these covered transactions must be published in one or more newspapers of general circulation, comments are solicited, and hearings may be held.
AML-BSA	All banks are on the frontline in combating money laundering and the financing of terrorism and other financial crimes. At the heart of **AML-BSA** is the requirement that banking institutions must establish and implement an effective AML-BSA program.[11] This program must be individually tailored to take into account the bank's size, complexity, geographic footprint, customer base, and products and services. At a minimum, the compliance program must contain the following elements, commonly known as the "four pillars:"[12] internal controls, independent testing, an independent BSA officer, and training.

10. 12 U.S.C. § 2902.

11. 31 U.S.C. §§ 5318(a)(2) and 5318(h). See, FFIEC BSA/AML Examination Manual.

12. 31 U.S.C. § 5318(h)(1); 12 U.S.C. § 1818(s); 12 C.F.R. §§ 21.21 (OCC); 208.63 (Federal Reserve); 326.8(c) (FDIC).

	As a part of the AML-BSA compliance program, each bank must implement a board of directors–approved written "Customer Identification Program" (**CIP**) that includes risk-based procedures to verify, to the extent reasonable and practicable, the identity of each of its customers.[13] These procedures must be based on the bank's assessment of the relevant risks, including those presented by the types of accounts maintained by the bank, methods of opening accounts provided by the bank, types of identifying information available, and the bank's size, location, and customer base.

The Differences

Second, the differences. The following are the general areas that we usually associate with this issue:

- activities and powers;
- preemption;
- supervisory fees;
- legislative responsiveness; and
- miscellaneous regulatory issues.

In a nutshell:

Activities
• National Banks—as indicated above, national banks have been permitted to engage in a broad range of activities that are part of, or incidental to, the business of banking, either directly or through an operating subsidiary. With respect to activities and powers, the only significant disadvantages of the national bank charter in comparison to most statechartered banks are that: (i) insurance agency operations must comply with Section 92 of the NBA, which requires that insurance be sold from a place with a population of 5,000 or less; and (ii) national banks lack the authority to act as a travel agency or real estate broker—agency activities that are available to some state banks under applicable state law.

13. 31 C.F.R. § 1020.220(a)(1).

- State Banks—These institutions are limited to powers of national banks, except agency activities (insurance agency, travel agent, real estate broker). Principal activities not permitted to national banks require the approval of the FDIC. For example, some state laws permit real estate development, ownership of stock, and operating insurance companies. Through the so-called "Wild Card" and "Super Wild Card" provisions of a number of state laws, those state-chartered banks may offer any product or service that can be legally offered by national banks, insured savings associations, or any other state-chartered banks in the United States, subject to the same limitations and restrictions established for the product or service by applicable law.

Preemption

- Historically, preemption has been one of the primary drivers of choosing a national bank charter. This perceived advantage arises because state-chartered banks are generally subject to the laws of the particular state or states in which they operate. National banks, however, are creatures of federal statute and are specifically exempted from state laws that obstruct, impair, or condition their ability to fully exercise deposit-taking, lending, and operational powers.
- State banks need to follow the laws of each state when branching into other states.

Reputation of the Regulator

- Various regulators have reputations and may be viewed as more flexible or more enforcement-minded.
- The proximity of the regulatory "region" can be important.
- State bank regulators and the FDIC are often seen as specializing in local/community banks.
- Responsiveness is key.

Costs

- Examination fees can be high, and states are cheaper than the OCC. The Federal Reserve and FDIC do not charge for examinations.
- Federal licensing fees are also high, and states are cheaper.
- State banks can opt out of Federal Reserve membership and avoid the costs of FRB stock purchase (national banks must be members).

Other Miscellaneous Differences

- Lending Limits—state bank lending limits may be less restrictive than those for national banks (see Chapter 7).
- Investments—State member banks and national banks must adhere to investment limits set forth in 12 C.F.R. Part 1, which essentially limits investments to high-grade debt obligations. Nonmember bank investment rules are under state law and may be less restrictive.
- Dividend Payment—Without prior OCC approval, a national bank may not pay dividends in any calendar year that, in the aggregate, exceed the bank's year-to-date net income plus the bank's retained net income for the two preceding years. State laws differ and may be more or less restrictive.

4

The Corporate Family

Meet the Corporate Family

As can be seen from the discussions in the preceding chapters, you cannot find the applicable law to respond to an issue raised by a banking client unless you identify the charter and regulators of that client. Seldom will you discover that your client is only one entity. So, it is not only the bank charter that should concern you, but also the other members of the family: the parent (holding company), children (subsidiaries), and sisters and brothers (commonly controlled financial institutions and nonbank companies).

The following is an example of a bank corporate family, depicting affiliate options:

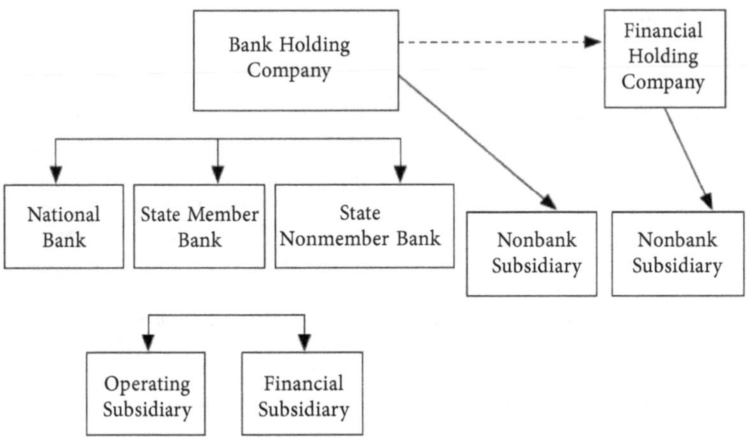

While there is no "rule" in this regard, the common practice of bankers and their lawyers is to create a bank family chart like the above example and depict the banking entities owned by the parent company on the left side (as we look at the chart) and the nonbank entities on the right, with arrows to show ownership.

Do all bank families look like this? Of course not. Some may be just a bank and a subsidiary or just a holding company owning one bank. Large banks may have dozens of subsidiaries with their own subsidiaries, so the chart goes down vertically through many levels.

Holding Companies

A large number of banks and thrifts in this country have parent holding companies. Originally, holding companies were utilized almost exclusively to avoid legal restrictions on banks, including both geographic and activity-related restrictions. As such, they came under fire by regulators and eventually came under the scrutiny of Congress, which led to restrictions, compliance obligations, and regulatory supervision.

Bank Holding Companies

Today's bank holding companies (**BHCs**) may be large global conglomerates, or they may be parent companies of community banks. They are state-chartered corporations or limited liability companies that control one or more banks and are federally regulated by the Federal Reserve. The primary business of BHCs has historically been the management and control of banks.

Applicable Statutory Law. The BHCA contains most of the federal law applicable to BHCs. It, like many federal banking statutes, is definitionally driven, and understanding the terms and the organization is critical to understanding the law.

The BHCA is organized such that:
***Section 2** includes the definitions that are so crucial to understanding the law;*
***Section 3** deals with the formation of BHCs, merger of BHCs, and BHC acquisitions of banks; and*
***Section 4** focuses on "nonbanking" activities and provides the infamous activity restrictions. (By the way, Section 4 applies to BHC acquisitions of savings associations, not Section 3.)*
When you try to find these sections in the codified version of the BHCA in the U.S.C., they are each one number less than the section number; accordingly, Section 2 is found at 12 U.S.C. § 1841; Section 3 is § 1842; and Section 4 is § 1843.

Applicable Regulation. The implementing Federal Reserve regulation under the BHCA is Regulation Y. "Y" is the 25th letter in the alphabet, so you will find it at 12 C.F.R. Part 225.

When Is a Company a BHC? Any *company* (broadly defined in Section 2 of the BHCA) that *controls* (defined with great complexity in Section 2 and numerous Federal Reserve pronouncements) a *bank* (as defined in Section 2 to include any FDIC-insured depository institution, except savings associations) is governed by the BHCA and must apply to the Federal Reserve as such. This area is literally a book on its own in the context of funds and other professional investors in banks who seek to not be BHCs. For the most part though, our client BHCs own 100 percent of the stock of one or more banks.

Ownership of Banks. All the rules on BHC ownership of banks are found in Section 3 of the BHCA. Assume there will be an application for any covered transaction.

Activities. Holding companies conduct most nonbanking activities through subsidiary organizations that may be wholly owned or partially owned by the parent. The holding company and the nonbank subsidiaries are the quintessential "affiliates" of banks for the purposes of prudential regulation (the subject of Chapter 7), in contrast to operating subsidiaries discussed below.

BHCs and their nonbanking subsidiaries are unlimited in geographic scope but strictly restricted on the activities in which they may engage by virtue of Section 4(c) of the BHC. Section 4 has some interesting twists, such as:

- permitting BHCs to own 5% or less of any company [Section 4(c)(2)] (famous for permitting SunTrust to own 5% of Coca Cola); and
- permitting a company to acquire a BHC and keep illegal activities for a period of 2 years, with extensions [Section 4(c)(6)] (famous for permitting Travelers Insurance to acquire Citicorp many years ago when the transaction was otherwise illegal).

But the key provision is Section 4(c)(8), which limits BHCs to activities "closely related to banking and a proper incident thereto." For decades, the Federal Reserve construed this language, issuing interpretations and approvals as it built the list of "**4(c)(8) activities**" and deposited the list in Regulation Y at 12 C.F.R. § 225.28. (Suffice it to say that the items on the list do not materially diverge from what banks can do, except in connection with securities activities.) This expansion was suspended, maybe permanently, by Gramm-Leach-Bliley when the list was "frozen" as of November 11, 1999. Thus, there will be no further expansion of Section 4(c)(8) absent Congressional intervention, and BHCs that do not qualify as financial holding companies (**FHCs**) must continue to operate under these restrictions.

> *To find out those activities in which a BHC may engage, you need merely to look at the list in* § 225.28 *and then follow up with the interpretive letters to obtain context and specifics.*

Holding Companies that Are not Regulated as BHCs

There are specialized banks, such as credit card banks and ILCs, that are excluded from the definition of "bank" for purposes of the BHCA. Companies that control these banks are therefore not BHCs and are not subject to the Section 4(c)(8) activity restrictions of the BHCA, or to the restrictions for FHCs. They also are not subject to Federal Reserve regulation and supervision. Department stores and manufacturing firms have used this avenue into banking. There are several other bells and whistles but essentially the banks may not accept demand deposit accounts and make commercial loans. The exceptions are in Section 2 of the BHCA at definitions (F) and (H).

Financial Holding Companies

Financial holding companies (**FHCs**) are not separate entities. They are BHCs that certify with the Federal Reserve and are permitted a broader range of activities that are "financial in nature" or "incidental" or "complementary" thereto.

> *Even though an FHC has special powers and rights, it is still a BHC and is subject to all laws and regulations applicable to BHCs, except as otherwise provided in Section 4 (primarily in regard to activities and applications).*

Activities. FHCs are governed by Sections 4(k)-(o) of the BHCA. Their expanded permissible activities are under Section 4(k) (so, that is 12 U.S.C. § 1843(k), based on what you learned above), and include:

- underwriting, dealing, and making a market in securities;
- acting as an agent, broker, or principal in connection with insurance;
- merchant banking or venture capital;
- mutual fund activities (advisor, distributor, administrator, seller, sponsor);
- securities lending, safeguarding, exchanging;
- issuing or selling asset-backed securities;
- travel agency;
- pension fund administrator; and
- underwriting and dealing in foreign government debt.

Incidental and complementary activities must be approved by the Board. Being a "finder" is an example of an incidental activity.

Applications. One practical advantage of FHC status is that an FHC may acquire most nonbank entities without the prior approval of the Board. There are no applications, just an after-the-fact filing, except to acquire IDIs, which are done under Section 3 of the BHCA and do require applications.

Prerequisites. BHCs seeking to be FHCs must qualify to engage in the new activities. In essence, they must be the "best and brightest." To qualify they must certify to the Board that:

- the BHC and its IDI subsidiaries are "**well capitalized**" and "**well managed**;"
- the subsidiary IDI(s) must have a CRA rating of at least "Satisfactory."

> *You will see these terms used frequently in this book.*
> *They are bellwethers for sound financial institutions.*
> *A "well-capitalized institution" meets high capital requirements discussed in Chapter 6;*
> *a "well-managed institution" earns good examination ratings, as discussed in Chapter 8; and*
> *CRA "satisfactory" means examiners determined the IDIs are meeting the needs of their community.*

An FHC may lose its status if it becomes less than "well capitalized" or if it is rated as less than "well managed." There is generally a 180-day cure period after notice from the Federal Reserve, or a longer period as prescribed by the agency. If the violation is not cured, the FHC must stop engaging in activities other than activities otherwise permissible for a BHC.

Thrift Holding Companies

A thrift holding company is any company that directly or indirectly controls a federal or state savings association under HOLA and the Savings and Loan Holding Company Amendments of 1967.[1] These holding companies in stock form are general business corporations incorporated under state law; they may be in mutual form, and, in fact, most were historically. These entities were regulated primarily at the federal level by the OTS. Thrift holding companies are now regulated and examined by the Federal Reserve. Existing OTS regulations, as amended in some respects, were moved to the Federal Reserve's Regulation LL and MM on July 21, 2011.

1. Publ. L. 90-255, Feb. 14, 1967, 82 Stat. 5.

> *The alphabet has 26 letters, so you go to "Z" and then to LL (the 12th letter) and arrive at 38. That makes Regulation LL 12 C.F.R. Part 238 and MM Part 239. (I literally have to think this way.)*

Activities. The scope of permissible activities of thrift holding companies and their nonbank affiliates depended historically on whether the holding company was "**unitary**"—owning one thrift—or "multiple"—owning more than one thrift. A unitary holding company was permitted to engage in any commercial activity; a multiple was limited to bank holding company activities with a few extras tossed in. The expanded authority of unitaries was eliminated by Section 401 of Gramm-Leach-Bliley as of May 4, 1999.[2] Under this provision, all thrift holding companies approved after May 4, 1999, could engage in activities that were financial in nature or incidental or complementary thereto, like FHCs.

Today, all thrift holding companies may exercise FHC powers, subject to the conditions and limits imposed by the Federal Reserve. Any pre-Gramm-Leach-Bliley unitary thrift holding company that met the test as a unitary continues to be essentially restriction-free as to activities. It may be a manufacturer or a department store or an insurance underwriter, and it may add activities willy-nilly.

Credit Unions

The following is a test: Can a member-owned entity have a parent company? Although they figured out a way with mutual savings associations, not so for credit unions.

The Significance of Size

Holding companies come in many sizes, and the size makes a difference in connection with the application of some laws, capital requirements, and in the degree of Federal Reserve oversight. The following highlights the importance of various sizes.

2. Section 401 amended 10(c) of HOLA, adding (9)(C) (12 U.S.C. § 1467a(c)(9)(C)).

Type of Holding Company	Asset Size	Significance
Regional BHCs and THCs	$10 billion and greater	<u>*Interchange Fees*</u> (12 C.F.R. Part 235)—The Durbin Amendment to Dodd-Frank required the Federal Reserve to establish a maximum permissible interchange fee for many types of debit transactions. Interchange (or "swipe") fees are charges that merchants pay to card-issuing banks for processing electronic payment transactions. The Federal Reserve set the maximum interchange fee at 21 cents plus five basis points (0.05%) of the transaction value. <u>*Volcker Rule*</u> (e.g., 12 C.F.R. Part 248)—The so-called "Volcker Rule" (also a part of Dodd-Frank) restricts the ability of banking entities (holding companies and their affiliates) with $10 billion in assets or greater to sponsor or invest in private funds or to engage in certain types of proprietary trading. <u>*CFPB Examination and Enforcement*</u>—The CFPB has examination and enforcement authority over banks and thrifts with more than $10 billion in assets (measured over four consecutive quarters).
Formerly Systemically Important	$50 billion to $100 billion	These companies and banks were relieved of the burden associated with being labeled systemically important in the Regulatory Relief Act.
"Mega" Regionals	$100 billion to $250 billion	These companies and banks were also relieved of the label systemically important, but the Federal Reserve has tailoring rules for "**enhanced prudential standards**" based on risk. They must stress-test capital on a two-year cycle and stress-test liquidity quarterly. They also must submit capital plans annually.

Systemically Important	$250 billion and greater	These institutions are considered systemically important and are subject to the enterprise-wide supervision of the Federal Reserve. They are subject to the enhanced prudential standards (12 C.F.R. Part 252), which include capital planning and both company-run and supervisory-run stress testing, liquidity risk management and stress testing, single counterparty credit limits, and enterprise risk management.[3]
G-SIBs	Identified as "globally systemically important" (8 U.S. BHCs)	The largest institutions are subject to additional constraints and capital surcharges.

The Federal Reserve provides a chart detailing the requirements and standards for each of the tailoring categories of banking organizations at https://www.federalreserve.gov/aboutthefed/boardmeetings/files/tailoring-rule-visual-20191010.pdf.

Consequences of Being a Bank or Thrift Holding Company

Why do banks and thrifts have holding companies? For many it was about having a corporation that could go to market to sell stock and be able to borrow with bank stock as collateral—and be able to do both without worrying about a bank regulator refereeing. The reason our community bank clients formed BHCs back in the 1980's was primarily to facilitate the market for their stock by engaging in stock repurchases.

The following are often-cited reasons:

- BHCs may offer a full suite of financial products, including loans, deposits, securities brokerage services, investment advisory and wealth management services, and investment products.
- BHCs facilitate multi-state operations.

3. *Prudential Standards for Large Bank Holding Companies, Savings and Loan Holding Companies, and Foreign Banking Organizations* (Nov. 1, 2019), https://www.federalregister.gov/documents/2019/11/01/2019-23662/prudential-standards-for-large-bank-holding-companies-savings-and-loan-holding-companies-and-foreign

- By owning multiple banks, BHCs may offer depositors increased deposit insurance benefits.
- BHCs facilitate better risk management and corporate organization: e.g., managers can separate the retail bank from credit card operations or wholesale bank operations, or higher risk lending from lower risk lending.

That said, there are serious consequences:

Limited Entry	Any bank or thrift may form a holding company by application to the Federal Reserve as governed by Section 3 of the BHCA. However, when someone wants to buy an interest in a bank, it encounters complications and barriers to entry from control issues and application requirements.
Limited Powers	FHCs and THCs have broad financial powers, as indicted above, but BHCs are limited to the list in Regulation Y.
Consolidated Capital	All holding companies, except those under $3 billion in assets and those that elect the Community Bank Leverage Ratio, must comply with Basel III capital requirements on a consolidated basis, as discussed in Chapter 6.
Source of Strength	This is the real barrier. The Federal Reserve embraced a policy for many years referred to as the "source of strength doctrine" that obligated BHCs to act as a source of financial and managerial strength to depository institution subsidiaries and to commit resources to support such subsidiaries in circumstances where the BHC might not otherwise do so. The policy was made law for BHCs and THCs as a result of Section 616(d) of Dodd-Frank[4] and goes all the way to the top company in a financial institution family. Dodd-Frank defines the term as "the ability of a company that directly or indirectly owns or controls an insured depository institution to provide financial assistance to such insured depository institution in the event of the financial distress of the insured depository institution."

4. Codified at Section 38A of the FDIA (12 U.S.C. § 1831). See also 12 C.F.R. § 225.4(a) and 12 C.F.R. § 238.8, the Board's source of strength regulations for BHCs and THCs, respectively.

<table>
<tr><td>Anti-tying</td><td>Product tying is prohibited between the bank/thrift and the holding company and its affiliates under Section 106 of the BHCA.[5] Unless an exception applies, "tying" means offering a bank loan or other bank product or service or varying the consideration on a bank loan or other bank product or service on any of the following conditions:
<ul>
<li>the customer's obtaining another product or service from a bank or its affiliate; or</li>
<li>the customer's providing some additional credit, property, or service to the bank or its affiliates; or</li>
<li>the customer's agreeing not to obtain credit, property, or services from a competitor.</li>
</ul>
In 2003, the Board published its explanation of how it views the tying restrictions and the exemptions. The release provides a road map for this area of law: See, Antitying Restrictions of Section 106 of the Bank Holding Company Act Amendments of 1970: Proposed interpretation and supervisory guidance with request for public comment, 68 Fed. Reg. 52,024 (Aug. 29, 2003).</td></tr>
</table>

Bank Subsidiaries

Virtually every activity engaged in by financial institutions, except deposit-taking, which requires a bank charter, may be conducted in a subsidiary of the institution. For a variety of business reasons, banks and thrifts may select a subsidiary structure for:

Marketing purposes	because a subsidiary will use a nonbank name that may be more readily identifiable with the product
Operational purposes	because a subsidiary operates as a separate corporation with its own, often specialized, board of directors and officers

5. Pub. L. 91-607, title I, § 106(b), Dec. 31, 1970, 84 Stat. 1766, (12 U.S.C. § 1972). The Board's tying rules are published at 12 C.F.R. § 225.7.

Liability-containment purposes	because a subsidiary, which appropriately conducts its activities separate and apart from those of the parent bank, will contain its liabilities and not expose the parent bank's assets and capital

Moreover, there are legal reasons that may force the use of a subsidiary. For instance, there are structures that require subsidiary usage for bank regulatory reasons, such as certain partnerships and joint ventures.

What Is a Subsidiary?

Subsidiaries are entities that are wholly owned or *controlled* by a depository institution. There are a number of different types of financial institution subsidiaries, some of which provide institutions with the opportunity to engage in activities that they cannot engage in directly, such as real estate development for savings associations. Others provide operational flexibility by giving institutions a choice of conducting activities in a subsidiary or in the bank itself.

Principal Kinds of Subsidiaries

The regulatory agencies recognize the following subsidiary structures:

Subsidiary Structure	Description
Operating Subsidiaries	These are corporations or similar entities that may engage in activities in which the bank or savings association may engage in directly. As a regulatory matter, traditional operating subsidiaries are treated for the most part as separately incorporated divisions of the parent bank and, as such, are treated like banks, not as affiliates, for the purposes of many prudential regulations.
Bank Service Companies	These companies can be organized and controlled by one or more depository institutions to perform services for banks and other depository institutions, including credit unions.

Statutory Subsidiaries	These are companies in which banks are authorized to invest by law, such as bank service companies, small business development corporations, safe deposit companies, companies that hold the premises of the bank, and, for national banks and state member banks, Edge Act and agreement corporations for foreign investment.
"Section 24" Subsidiaries	These are subsidiaries of state banks that may engage in activities that are prohibited for subsidiaries of national banks, if approved by the FDIC under Section 24 of the FDIA.[6]
Service Corporations	These are subsidiaries of savings associations and credit unions (called "**CUSOs**" for credit union service organizations), not banks, which have broader powers than the parent.
Financial Subsidiaries	These are subsidiaries in which banks may provide most of the financial services not permissible for the bank itself, such as general securities underwriting, that are authorized for FHCs. They may not underwrite insurance or engage in merchant banking. For a bank to own a financial subsidiary, it must be well capitalized, well managed, and compliant with the CRA. It also must meet several additional prudential safeguards under 12 C.F.R. § 5.39(g).

Thrift Subsidiary Organizations

Savings associations may operate indirectly through two types of subordinate organizations in which they invest: *service corporations*, which are entities either formed as subsidiaries or as joint ventures, are permitted to engage in activities reasonably related to the activities of federal associations as the OCC may determine and approve.[7] This authority is contrasted to *operating subsidiaries* of federal associations, which are more akin to departments of associations, albeit separately incorporated.

Operating Subsidiaries. Operating subsidiaries of federal associations may be organized in any state and may conduct any activity that the parent federal association may conduct after notifying the OCC of the creation of the subsidiary. The association must control 50% or more of the voting shares of the subsidiary, and no other entity may exercise operating control.

6. 12 U.S.C. § 1831a.

7. 12 U.S.C. § 1464(c)(4)(B); 12 C.F.R. § 5.59.

OCC regulations on operating subsidiaries of savings associations are found at 12 C.F.R. § 5.38.

Service Corporations. A federal association may invest up to 3% of its assets in one or more service corporations as long as the excess investment over 2% serves primarily community, inner city, or community and economic development needs or public welfare purposes consistent with 12 C.F.R. § 24. OCC regulations on service corporations of savings associations are found at 12 C.F.R. § 5.59.

Service corporations are corporations chartered under state law, but the OCC will consider applications to organize a first-tier service corporation as an LLC or a limited partnership on a case-by-case basis. First-tier service corporation ownership is limited to associations that have their home office in the state in which the corporation is chartered and are organized under the laws of the home state.

Noncontrolling Investments in Subsidiaries

Originally all subsidiaries had to be "controlled" in order for the investment to be permissible. Otherwise, the bank was making an impermissible equity investment in an entity. However, the historical resistance has given way, and banks may make noncontrolling investments in "subsidiaries" under strict rules.

National Banks

Subject to certain conditions, the Comptroller permits national banks to make noncontrolling investments in companies that engage in activities permitted to national banks upon 10 days after-the-fact notice to the OCC.[8] National banks must be well capitalized and well managed in order to take advantage of the after-the-fact notice. Generally, a national bank may make the noncontrolling investment either directly or through an operating subsidiary.

State Banks

The investments of state banks are determined by state law with federal law overlaid. As discussed above, state banks may not make any equity investment directly or indirectly of a type not permitted for national banks without FDIC approval.[9] Thus, noncontrolling investments by state banks would fall within the FDICIA rule and be tied to national bank authority

8. 12 C.F.R. § 5.36(e).
9. 12 C.F.R. § 362.3(a).

and would be subject to a Federal Reserve policy that less than 100% owned subsidiaries of state banks must comply with Section 4(c)(8) of the BHCA (another historical anomaly). Further, states may impose more restrictive conditions, and state banks would have to follow the application or notice requirements of their respective state regulator.

Savings Associations

Federal savings associations have the authority to invest in service corporations in any amount, so noncontrolling investments are contemplated for federal associations and are, thus, permitted for state associations unless otherwise provided by applicable state law.

5

Understanding a Bank through Its Financial Statements

The Business of Banking

Bank lawyers need to understand the basic business of banking in order to talk to their clients and give them sound legal and risk advice. This book gives you bits and pieces of the business as it meanders through the legal essentials, but not really enough. As an educator, I have found we can shortcut this assignment by studying simplified financial statements of a prototypical commercial bank. One of the many lawyers with whom I had the pleasure of teaching banking law created this exercise many years ago and I continue to use it. Edward Lane-Reticker has been gone from us for a long time, but his "ProtoBank" lives on.

Financial Statements

The basic financial statements of IDIs include:

- a Statement of Condition or Balance Sheet, which shows the solvency of the IDI at a given point in time (end of quarter or end of fiscal year); and
- an Income Statement, which shows profitability over the course of the quarter or year.

All IDIs are required by law to prepare these statements, along with a slew of other reports and schedules, for regulators and the public. Going back in history, IDIs "called" their financial results into the regulators and the reports became known as **"Call"** Reports. Call Reports are filed quarterly and annually with the IDI's primary federal regulator.

The FDIC publishes all Call Report information for FDIC-insured institutions, and you can look banks up on the ***Federal Financial Institutions Examination Council*** *(FFIEC) website:*

https://cdr.ffiec.gov/public/ManageFacsimiles.aspx

In addition, publicly held holding companies file consolidated financial statements with the Securities and Exchange Commission (**SEC**)—quarterly reports on Form 10-Q and annual reports on Form 10-K.

Look up financial statements on EDGAR:
https://www.sec.gov/edgar/searchedgar/companysearch.html

Enter the company name and search for the most recent 10-K, which also includes a "Supervision and Regulation" discussion—a must read for bank regulatory lawyers!

ProtoBank Statement of Condition

Here is the Statement of Condition/Balance Sheet of ProtoBank.
Note:

- Assets (what the IDI "owns" or are "owed to it") are always on the left.
- Liabilities (what the IDI "owes") are the source of bank funds and are always on the right.
- The two columns end up with the same sum (hence the name "Balance Sheet").
- The balancing factor is capital, which is the focus of Chapter 6.

This Balance Sheet is presented in "billions" of dollars, so add lots of zeroes to each number. Which means, ProtoBank is a $10 billion commercial bank—a mid-range community bank.

PROTOBANK, N.A.
Statement of Condition
(in Billions)

Assets		**Liabilities & Capital**	
Cash & Due from Banks[1]	$0.8	Deposits[7, 8]	
Investments[2, 3]	2.2	Demand Deposits	$2.0
Loans[4]		NOW Accounts	1.4
Gross	6.65		
ALLL	0.15[5]	Money Market Accounts	2.3
Net Loans	6.5	Savings & Time Deposits	2.5
Trading Account Assets	.2	**Total Deposits**	**8.2**
Premises, Equipment & Other Assets[6]	.2	Trading Liabilities	.5
OREO	.0	Other Borrowing[9]	.5
Goodwill	.1	**Total Liabilities[10]**	**9.2**
		Capital[11]	0.8
Total Assets	**$10.0**	**Total Liabilities & Capital**	**$10.0**

Assets

Simplistically, banks buy and sell money as their core business. You will thus note that 96% of the bank's assets are financial assets, not physical assets. That concentration is actually a hint at a legal matter—banks are legally restricted in the tangible assets they may own.

The assets on the Balance Sheet are presented in order from the most "liquid" (cash) to the least liquid (tangible property). "Liquidity" refers to a bank's ability to meet its deposit and other obligations as they become due. The assets above are footnoted to match the descriptions below:

1. Cash & Due from Banks. This is the bank's primary liquidity reserve, the cash in its vaults, in its tellers' drawers, or on deposit with other banks (including Federal Reserve Banks). These are the funds that are immediately available to pay deposit and other obligations.
   a. No bank is liquid in the sense of being able to meet all of its obligations if they were presented at one time. While they are not likely to be presented at one time, IDIs have failed because they could not meet their liquidity needs.

   b. The law of large numbers, reinforced by deposit insurance and the safety net of the Federal Reserve System, makes it possible for banks to operate with fractional reserves (liquidity reserves that are only a small fraction of their liabilities).
   c. **Up until 2020, all IDIs had to maintain a certain percentage of "transaction account" deposits as fractional reserves set aside at the local Federal Reserve Bank as required by the FRA and Regulation D. Reserve amounts are accounted for in the Cash and Due from Banks item. In 2020, the Federal Reserve determined that we were operating in an "ample reserve environment" and reduced reserve legal requirements to zero. (That does not mean IDIs don't need reserves. It just means the Federal Reserve does not dictate what they must hold.)**
2. <u>Investments</u>. The investment portfolio is the bank's secondary liquidity reserve because it consists, or should consist, of investments that, for the most part, may be quickly liquidated and converted to cash to pay deposit and other obligations.
   a. Investments must be "**bank eligible**," meaning they are expressly permitted by applicable law. With few exceptions, the investments will be **debt instruments**, such as bonds or notes that are regularly quoted and readily marketable. They will usually be government obligations: federal, state, or municipal. They may also include high-grade corporate debt instruments.
   b. With some exceptions, they do not include stock or other equity investments. Banks do not have the power to speculate in the securities markets.
   c. The three most important aspects of a bank's investment portfolio for regulatory purposes are: (i) the size of the portfolio relative to the bank's liabilities; (ii) the credit quality of the obligors; and (iii) the average maturity or duration of the instruments. The shorter the maturity, the nearer the market value of the investment or loan will be to its book value and the more likely it will be that it can be liquidated without substantial loss. Investments are grouped as "**available for sale**" and "**held to maturity**." The former are marked-to-market on an ongoing basis whereas the later may be valued using a more flexible measure.
3. <u>Investments and Loans</u>. In a basic sense, bank investments and bank loans are really the same thing, loans by the bank to borrowers.
   a. However, a loan is usually a "one of a kind" transaction, with the amount, maturity, and other terms worked out by agreement between the bank and the borrower. Its value is a matter of judgment, which depends on the credit worthiness of the borrower,

the maturity, and other factors. It is not readily marketable and therefore illiquid.

   b. In the case of an investment, the bank lends its money by purchasing bonds, notes, or other debt securities issued by the borrower, which is usually a government or a business corporation. The debt obligations are issued in standard denominations, such as $10,000. The current market values of the obligations are quoted regularly in the financial press, and they are readily marketable through brokers and dealers. Investments are a source of liquidity, while loans generally are not, although loans may be turned into securities through securitization.

4. Loans. Both "gross" and "net" loans appear on the Balance Sheet. The difference is the amount that the bank has set aside for anticipated credit losses.
5. Allowance for Loan and Lease Losses (**ALLL**). (Also called loan loss reserve, bad debt reserve, etc.) Loan and lease losses are charged against the ALLL, and the ALLL is replenished from the "Provision for Loan and Lease Losses," which appears on the Income Statement. Note, the ALLL is subtracted from Gross Loans and that is the only subtracted amount on the Balance Sheet. That is known as a "**contra account**" because it is contrary to the flow of the assets.
6. Premises, Equipment & Other Assets. Fixed assets usually make up only a small part of a bank's assets, only 4% in ProtoBank's case.
   a. Banks have legal limitations on the fixed assets they may own, typically only as necessary for the operation of the business.
   b. They may only own real property for their main offices and branches and, to some extent, for future growth. While some state banks and savings and loan associations may legally own real estate to develop, it is on a limited basis and the general rule is they may not speculate on land.
   c. "**OREO**" means Other Real Estate Owned. This is property the bank forecloses on, and they may hold it for approximately 3 years, with the possibility of extensions.

Liabilities and Capital

These are the funds the bank uses in its business: borrowed in the case of liabilities, and supplied by shareholders or retained from earnings in the case of capital.

7. Deposits. **A deposit is a loan to the bank by a depositor, and depositors are creditors of the bank**. Contrast that with a money market mutual fund where the customer is a shareowner of the fund.
   a. A deposit represents the liability of the bank to repay the depositor, either on demand or at the time agreed. The bank invests the

deposited funds, and relends them to its borrowers, or puts them into its liquidity reserve. The investments, the loans, and the cash belong to the bank, not to the depositors. That is what makes banks "financial intermediaries," not agents—they take your money and book it as theirs.

b. Deposits are the bank's principal liability and its principal source of funds. Different types of deposits have different maturities and other terms, may pay different interest rates, and may require different reserves. If a bank is liquidated, deposits have priority over other unsecured liabilities.

8. Deposit Account Types. Historically, the definition of accounts that were "transaction accounts" was a critical component of Regulation D because those accounts were essentially payable upon demand and required the bank to hold reserves against them. As noted above, the establishment by law of reserve requirements is a thing of the past.
   a. Demand deposits (regular checking) accounts (**DDAs**) are corporate and individual transaction accounts. They permit immediate withdrawal and are used for payments.
   b. **NOW** (Negotiable Order of Withdrawal) accounts are a special type of transaction account. Like a savings account they pay interest, and like a checking account, they may be used for payments. They are not available to businesses.
   c. Money Market Deposit Accounts (**MMDA**s) are a type of savings account that pays interest and historically permitted a limited number of transactions. They were originally intended to permit the payment of a rate competitive with the return on money market mutual funds. IDIs must disclose the right to hold funds for 7 days before payment.
   d. Savings & Time Deposits include deposits that permit withdrawal but not check transactions—savings accounts—and deposits that have fixed maturities—certificates of deposit (**CDs**). For savings accounts (like with MMDAs), IDIs must disclose the right to hold funds for 7 days before payment.

   In the new "ample reserves environment," these definitions are becoming irrelevant. Nevertheless, IDIs tend to maintain the distinctions in their product offerings.

9. Other Borrowing. Other borrowing includes (a) long-term borrowing that for some regulatory purposes may count as capital, and (b) short-term borrowing (such as "**federal funds**" transactions and other money market borrowing). Borrowing may enable an IDI to make loans and investments when deposits are insufficient, or to repay deposits if cash reserves are inadequate.

10. Total Liabilities. Deposits and other borrowing combined.

11. Capital. Capital or Net Worth is the difference between the IDI's assets and its liabilities. These funds have been supplied by the shareholders or are retained from earnings. If the IDI's assets shrink, its capital provides a "cushion" to absorb losses and protect the bank's depositors, other lenders, and the FDIC. The importance of capital is the subject of Chapter 6.
    a. Note that the amount of ProtoBank's capital, like that of most banks, is small in relation to its total assets. Depositors and other lenders have provided 92% of the funds that the bank is using. Shareholders have provided only 8%, Thus, if the bank loses as little as 8% of its assets (through imprudent investments or loans, or a mismatch between the interest rates for assets and liabilities, etc.), its capital will be exhausted and it will be on the verge of insolvency. Any further deterioration will result in loss to depositors or lenders, or the FDIC to the extent that deposits are insured.
    b. Capital may be classified into subcategories such as capital, paid-in surplus, earned surplus, and retained earnings; or into common stock and one or more classes of preferred stock. These categories can be important for the purposes of corporate law and the relative rights of different classes of shareholders.
12. Leverage. "Leverage" refers to the ratio of debt to equity. A leverage ratio of 10:1 means that the bank has ten times as much debt as equity.
    a. High leverage is a characteristic of banks. Banks operate with much less capital than industrial and commercial firms, where even a leverage ratio of 1:1 would be considered high. The term is a metaphor—indicating that a small amount of capital can support a large amount of lending and investing. Leverage acts as an incentive for bank managements to accept more risk than managers in most other businesses.
    b. Because of leverage, a small amount of capital can generate large returns on investment. As you will see from the Income Statement below, ProtoBank has a 1.1% return on assets and 13.75% return on equity; but if ProtoBank could raise its return on assets from 1.1% to 2.1%, it's return on equity would nearly double, from 13.75% to 26.25%. Similarly, leverage is an incentive to operate with as little capital as possible. If ProtoBank's capital was only 4% of assets instead of 8%, its return on equity would be twice as great, 27.5% instead of 13.75%. If ProtoBank both increased its return on assets to 2.1% and reduced its capital to 4%, the combination would increase its return on equity to 52.5%.

ProtoBank Income Statement

Here is the Income Statement of ProtoBank.
Note: Because the business of banks is to buy and sell money,

- the most important aspect of income is the interest earned on sold money, and
- the most important aspect of expense is interest paid on borrowings.

As a result, these amounts are reported and netted first.
This Statement of Income is presented in millions of dollars.

PROTOBANK, N.A.
Income Statement[1]
(in Millions)

Interest Income on Earning Assets[2]		$640
Interest Expense[3]		
Interest on Deposits[4]	150	
Interest on Other Borrowing[5]	40	
Total Interest Expense		(190)
Net Interest Income[6]		450
Provision for Loan and Lease Losses[7]		
For increase in loans outstanding	10	
For credit losses	15	
Total Loan Loss Provision		(25)
Net Interest Income after Provision for Loan Losses[8]		425
Non-Interest Income (Fees, etc.)[9]		190
Net Interest Income plus Non-Interest Income		615
Non-Interest Expense[10]		(450)
(Employee compensation and benefits, occupancy, services, depreciation, etc.)		
Income before taxes		165
Federal and State Taxes (33%)		(55)
Net Income[11]		$110

1. Note the structure of the Income Statement.
   a. Interest Income less Total Interest Expense equals Net Interest Income. Net Interest Income less the Total Provision for Loan and Lease Losses equals Net Interest Income after the Provision.
   b. The second part of the Income Statement adds Non-Interest Income and subtracts Non-Interest Expense to arrive at Income before Taxes. Finally, taxes are subtracted to arrive at Net Income.
2. ProtoBank's Earning Assets are its investments and loans, totaling $8.85 billion (Investments of $2.2 billion plus Gross Loans of $6.65 billion).
3. Interest Expense: The cost of borrowing the funds that the bank lends and invests.
4. Interest on Deposits: Interest on time and savings deposits. (The costs the bank incurs in servicing non-interest-bearing demand deposits (most checking accounts) are not included in "Interest Expense," but are a general operating expense and included in "non-interest expense.")
5. Interest on Other Borrowing: Note that the cost of these funds is much higher than the cost of deposit funds, 4% ($40 million/$1 billion) as compared with 2.4% ($150 million/$6.2 billion). The costs of servicing deposits and deposit insurance account for some of the difference.
6. Net Interest Income is the difference between "Interest Income" and "Total Interest Expense." "Net Interest Margin" is the difference between the average interest rate earned by the bank on all of its loans and investments ("earning assets") and the average interest rate paid by the bank on all of its interest-bearing deposits and borrowed funds.
7. Provision for Loan and Lease Losses is a deduction from "Net Interest Income" that provides for anticipated losses. The Provision appears on the Income Statement and is added to the ALLL, which appears on the Balance Sheet, and against which losses are charged. The "provision" is added to and replenishes the "allowance."
   a. The size of the ALLL reflects both external and internal considerations. **The new accounting method, Current Expected Credit Losses (CECL), is changing the way in which IDIs must assess future losses.** An IDI in an area where the economy is strong may not need as large an allowance as one in an area where the economy is showing signs of stress. An IDI with inadequate management and loan information systems will need a higher allowance than an IDI with a good system. If loans have grown from one period to the next, the ALLL will need to be increased if its ratio to outstanding loans is to be maintained at the previous level.
   b. Similarly, if loans have been charged off, the ALLL will need to be replenished if it is to be restored to its previous level. ProtoBank's Provision reflects both an increase in the level of loans outstanding

since the last accounting period and replenishment of the ALLL to compensate for credit losses that have been charged against it. (There has been some disagreement between bank regulators and the SEC about how certain or probable losses should be before they are provided for.)

c. The loss on a single loan may completely offset the income on many similar loans. For example, if a bank's loans have an average annual yield of 10%, a complete loss on a $1,000,000 loan will wipe out the earnings on ten good loans of the same size (in addition, of course, to the loss of interest on the defaulted loan).

8. Net Interest Income after Provision for Loan Losses. This is the bank's net income from its basic banking operations (borrowing and lending), before any administrative or operating expenses.
9. Non-Interest Income. In addition to interest income, ProtoBank earns income from other sources.
   This appears as "Non-Interest Income" on the Income Statement. This is a very important source of income for banks, especially when net interest margins are not strong. Some examples are service fees for account maintenance, fees for trust and custodial services, fees for commitments to extend credit, and rent from the leasing of space not currently needed by the bank. Also, sales of non-traditional products like insurance and securities result in non-interest income.
10. Non-Interest Expense. This is the expense of running the bank. The greatest part of it consists of employee compensation and benefits. Other costs are administrative expenses, account maintenance, rental payments for premises and equipment, and depreciation.
11. Net Income. Banks don't make much money relative to their size. Historically, a 1% return on assets has been a respectable performance, one often not achieved by large banks.

General Comments on the Business of Banking

As we wrap up this dive into financial statements, the following comments dot some i's and cross a few t's.

1. Loan Underwriting. Prudence, reinforced by regulation and supervision, requires careful initial and ongoing underwriting of loans. This includes proper authorization, documentation (current appraisals, current financial statements, guarantees, etc.), and record keeping. Continuous monitoring enables a bank to take remedial steps before losses becomes unavoidable. Examiners take a very close look at underwriting and even drill deep into portfolios and particular loans.
2. Yield Curve. As a general rule, the longer the term of a loan or debt instrument, the higher the interest rate—a rule often referred to as the

"yield curve." Because bank deposits are generally shorter in duration than bank loans, they ordinarily have lower interest rates. As a result, banks typically benefit from the "spread" between the lower cost of their funds and the higher return on their loans and investments.

3. Interest Rate Sensitivity. Because a bank's liabilities are generally of shorter duration than its assets, they reprice more quickly. Thus, a rise in the general level of interest rates will tend to increase a bank's cost of funds faster than its return on assets. At best, the result will be a squeeze on profit margins, or, at worst, large operating losses. If a loan portfolio is concentrated in long-term loans, sustained rise in interest rates can result in failure, as it did in the case of hundreds of thrifts in the Thrift Crisis of the 1980s.

6

Capital Basics

Identifying Capital

Regulatory capital represents the net assets of a banking organization—simplistically, we look at the balance sheet of a bank and subtract the liabilities from the assets and get "balance-sheet capital" (like our net worth when we subtract our personal liabilities from our assets). Capital is built first by investors purchasing securities and then is built by earnings.

Balance-sheet capital is referred to in financial statements as "**Shareholders' Equity**." Shareholders' Equity is broken down into the categories of instruments issued by the institution and purchased by shareholders and the related surplus (additional amounts paid by shareholders), plus all the earnings retained by the institution over its years of operations. The following table shows sample capital accounts for an institution with common stock and two kinds of preferred stock issued and outstanding.

Shareholders' Equity Example

Preferred Stock	$ (000 omitted)
8% non-cumulative perpetual—$25 par value; issued 500,000 shares	$ 12,500
8% cumulative perpetual—$25 par value; issued 1,750,000 shares	42,750
Common Stock, $1 par value—authorized 10,000,000 shares, issued 6,500,000 shares	6,500

Surplus	81,000
Retained Earnings	62,500
Total Shareholders' Equity	**$ 205,250**

Note: the dollars in the chart need to have 000 added for the real amounts (hence, the "000 omitted"). Thus, this institution has balance sheet capital of $205,250,000.

Capital Levels

Banks have been required to hold minimum levels of capital for safety and soundness purposes based on guidelines established by the bank regulatory agencies since 1983. The minimums have been expressed in terms of ratios of "capital" divided by "total assets." So, we always have a numerator (total capital) and a denominator (based on assets) that provides a ratio. Back when capital was easy, we divided capital by assets and the regulators said 8% was the objective. We lawyers could do the math!

The simplistic 8% capital requirement was ditched beginning in 1989 in favor of capital guidelines that were based upon international capital accords (known as "**Basel**" rules) adopted by the Basel Committee on Banking Supervision, a committee of central banks and bank supervisors that acts as the primary global standard-setter for prudential regulation, as implemented by the U.S. bank regulatory agencies on an interagency basis. (They meet in Basel, Switzerland, thus, the name.) The Committee recognized the critical importance of risk in banking and sought a method to calibrate capital to take into consideration the risks in the business of each depository institution. To that end, it recommended that bank assets for the purpose of the capital ratio calculations be "risk weighted" (the theory being that riskier assets should require more capital) and that off-balance sheet exposures needed to be factored into the calculations.

Following the Global Financial Crisis, the Group of Governors and Heads of Supervision, the oversight body of the Basel Committee, announced agreement on a strengthened set of capital requirements for banking organizations around the world, known as "**Basel III**," to address deficiencies recognized in connection with the crisis.

Suffice it to say, under the new capital regime, we lawyers no longer can do the math (thank goodness). To make the point, the following is a simple calculation in HTML (the PDF version is replete with the Greek letters):

max {0, [([Sigma]E - [Sigma]C) + [Sigma](Es x Hs) + [Sigma](Efx x Hfx)]{time}

The Basel III Rule

Basel III was an international recommendation that had to be adopted by each country's supervisors. It was "gold platted" (the U.S. likes to make things harder) and promulgated by each of our federal bank regulatory agencies in 2013 in the form of binding regulations. Basel III increased the required quantity and quality of capital and required more detailed categories of risk weighting of riskier, more opaque assets. For nearly every class of assets, the Basel III Rule requires a more complex, detailed, and calibrated assessment of risk.

Each of the federal banking agencies promulgated a nearly identical capital regulation that presents Basel III rules and the changes required by the Dodd-Frank Act:
Federal Reserve (for all holding companies and state member banks): 12 C.F.R. Part 217 (Regulation Q)

FDIC (for state nonmember banks and state savings associations): 12 C.F.R. Part 324

OCC (for national banks and federal thrifts): 12 C.F.R. Part 3

Basel III Calculations

Basel III favors several capital calculations. Thus, the numerator and denominator are now sliced and diced several ways.

Basel III Numerators. Because different kinds of equity have different levels of quality, what constitutes "capital" for regulatory purposes has different levels based on its ability to absorb loss:

Numerators	**Description**
Common Equity Tier 1 ("**CET 1**")	The purest form of capital that absorbs loss and cannot have any requirement for repayment. It includes the surplus and retained earnings.
Tier 1 Capital - CET 1 plus *Additional Tier 1*	Basically, adding non-cumulative perpetual preferred stock to CET 1.
Tier 2 Capital	Basically, adding other preferred stock, some forms of subordinated debt, and part of the allowance for loan and lease losses (**ALLL**).[1]
Total Capital	Tier 1 plus Tier 2.

1. The ALLL is a contra account on the bank's balance sheet (meaning you subtract it, instead of adding it like the rest of the balance sheet). It constitutes the reserve for bad debts that is determined by a bank's board of directors based on expected credit losses.

Now, look back up to the chart of Shareholders' Equity. The Common Stock and surplus and retained earnings are *CET 1*. Add the non-cumulative preferred stock as *Additional Tier 1* and that is *Tier 1*. The other preferred stock is *Tier 2* (as well as part of the ALLL). Total Capital is all of the above. (Note: there are other adjustments in Basel III that may apply.)

Basel III Denominators. There are also two different denominators that factor into the required ratios:

Denominator	Description
Risk-weighted assets	Assets are weighted according to risk and include off-balance sheet exposures brought back on the balance sheet based on risk. There are two approaches that determine the risk weighting: the **"Advanced Approach"** for the largest banking entities (basically $250 billion or more in consolidated assets) that use models and metrics for calculations and the **"Standardized Approach"** for all banking entities (it is a floor for Advanced Approaches institutions). For the standardized approach, each asset is assigned a risk factor. For instance, 50% is assigned for performing home mortgages. You find the risk weight by looking up the asset in Regulation Q.
Adjusted book assets	Assets are not risk weighted. The calculation uses total balance sheet assets, minus some intangibles.

Basel III Ratios. From these derive a number of different ratios:
CET 1 Capital to risk-weighted assets;
Tier 1 Capital to risk-weighted assets;
Total Capital to risk-weighted assets; and
Tier 1 Capital to adjusted book assets (known as the "**leverage ratio**").

Capital Adequacy

There are then several layers of capital adequacy.

Minimum Requirements

The adequacy of capital is first determined based on the **minimum** required. Under Basel III, the minimum capital ratios for all covered institutions as of January 1, 2015, are as follows:

Numerator	Denominator	Required Minimum Ratio
CET 1	risk-weighted assets	4.5%
Tier 1	risk-weighted assets	6%
Total Capital	risk-weighted assets	8%
Tier 1 "leverage ratio"	quarterly average balance sheet assets (with adjustments)	4%

Capital Conservation Buffer

But there is more. Institutions that seek the freedom to make capital distributions (including for dividends and repurchases of stock) and pay discretionary bonuses to executive officers without restriction must also maintain 2.5% of risk-weighted assets in CET 1 attributable to a "**Capital Conservation Buffer**." The purpose of the conservation buffer is to ensure that banking institutions maintain a buffer of capital that can be used to absorb losses during periods of financial and economic stress.

If an institution does not meet the 2.5% buffer, there is a graduated impact based on the amount of its buffer:

Common Equity Capital Conservation Buffer (as a percentage of risk-weighted assets)	Maximum payout ratio (as a percentage of eligible retained income)
Greater than 2.5%	No payout limitation applies
Greater than 1.875% and less than or equal to 2.5%	60%
Greater than 1.25% and less than or equal to 1.875%	40%
Greater than 0.625% and less than or equal to 1.25%	20%
Less than or equal to 0.625%	0%

Factoring in the full conservation buffer increases the minimum ratios depicted above to 7% for CET 1 Capital, 8.5% for Tier 1 Capital, and 10.5% for Total Capital.

To Be Well Capitalized

And there is more. To be "well capitalized," which is the regulatory objective, a banking organization must maintain no less than:

Numerator	Denominator	Required Minimum Ratio
CET 1	risk-weighted assets	6.5%
Tier 1	risk-weighted assets	8%
Total Capital	risk-weighted assets	10%
Tier 1	quarterly average balance sheet assets (with adjustments)	5%

It is possible under the Basel III Rule to be well capitalized while remaining out of compliance with the Capital Conservation Buffer mentioned above.

And there is still more for the largest banking institutions. They have countercyclical buffers and all kinds of surcharges and enhancements.

Prompt Corrective Action

The concept of an institution being "well capitalized" is part of a regulatory enforcement regime that provides the federal banking regulators with broad power to take "prompt corrective action" (**PCA**) to resolve the problems of depository institutions based on the capital level of each particular institution. The extent of the regulators' powers depends on whether the institution in question is "adequately capitalized," "undercapitalized," "significantly undercapitalized" or "critically undercapitalized," in each case as defined by regulation.

Depending upon the capital category to which an institution is assigned, the regulators' corrective powers include: (i) requiring the institution to submit a capital restoration plan; (ii) limiting the institution's asset growth and restricting its activities; (iii) requiring the institution to issue additional capital stock (including additional voting stock) or to sell itself; (iv) restricting transactions between the institution and its affiliates; (v) restricting the interest rate that the institution may pay on deposits; (vi) ordering a new election of directors of the institution; (vii) requiring that senior executive officers or directors be dismissed; (viii) prohibiting the institution from accepting deposits from correspondent banks; (ix) requiring the institution to divest certain subsidiaries; (x) prohibiting the payment of principal or interest on subordinated debt; and (xi) ultimately, appointing a receiver for the institution.

It should not be surprising to learn that each of the federal regulatory agencies adopted virtually identical PCA regulations:
Federal Reserve (for state member banks): 12 C.F.R. Part 208 (Regulation H), Appendix D
FDIC (for state nonmember banks and state savings associations): 12 C.F.R. Part 324, Subpart H
OCC (for national banks and federal thrifts): 12 C.F.R. Part 6

Application to the Corporate Family

Historically, concepts of capital adequacy applied only to IDIs. Thus, all commercial banks and all savings associations were under relatively uniform guidelines, but the parent companies, not so much. Recognizing once again that what worked before the Global Financial Crisis would not work going forward, Congress required that holding company capital requirements be the same as those applied to IDIs. As a result, capital is now measured on the individual depository institution and on the bank family as a consolidated group.

Community Bank Capital Simplification

Community banks have long raised concerns with bank regulators about the regulatory burden, complexity, and costs associated with certain provisions of Basel III. In response, Congress provided an "off ramp" for institutions with total consolidated assets of less than $10 billion. Section 201 of the Regulatory Relief Act instructed the federal banking regulators to establish a single "Community Bank Leverage Ratio" (**CBLR**) of between 8 and 10%. Under the final rule, a community banking organization is eligible to elect the new framework if it has: less than $10 billion in total consolidated assets, limited amounts of certain assets and off-balance sheet exposures, and a CBLR greater than 9%.

The Capital Consequences of Size

As indicated above, Basel III brought all U.S. FDIC-insured depository institutions and their holding companies under the same capital regime—sort of. But, there were carve-outs and surcharges, and, as time has gone by, turns out size matters—a lot!

	Asset Size	Significance
Small BHCs and THCs	Under \$3 billion	The "**Small BHC Policy Statement**"[2] of the Federal Reserve eliminates parent company capital requirements *as long as they do not*: engage in significant nonbanking activities, conduct significant off-balance sheet activities, or have a material amount of debt or equity securities registered with the SEC.
Small BHCs and THCs, Banks, and Savings Associations	Under \$10 billion	Have the option of an easier capital calculation under the CBLR.
Regional BHCs and THCs	Under \$15 billion	May retain certain kinds of capital, like non-conforming preferred stock and trust preferred securities that larger companies had to divest.
Advanced Approaches	\$250 billion and over	The U.S. BHCs that were permitted to use the second Basel capital accord, Basel II, to use metrics and models for determining risk weights and capital needs. They have to use the Standardized Approach (looking up the risk weight of the asset) as a floor. They also must hold a "**Countercyclical Capital Buffer.**"

2. *Available at* 12 C.F.R. Part 225, Appendix C.

G-SIBs	Identified as "globally systemically important" U.S. BHCs, by the Federal Reserve (Bank of America, Bank of New York, Citi, Goldman Sachs, J.P. Morgan Chase, Morgan Stanley, State Street, and Wells Fargo).	Subject to additional capital surcharges, including a G-SIB Surcharge, an Enhanced Supplemental Leverage Ratio, and, under consideration, a Stress Capital Buffer (to replace for them the Capital Conservation Buffer).

The Importance of Capital

Because capital is the difference between assets and liabilities, it acts as a buffer and the institution fails when it is depleted. When we view capital as lawyers (not from a macroeconomic perspective—we leave that to the Federal Reserve), we see that it acts in the following ways:

As a Loss Absorber

Capital has always been viewed first and foremost as a loss absorber. When a banking institution loses money on bad loans or investments, the loss reduces earnings and reduces assets such that both capital and the ability to rebuild capital decrease. All the bank crises through the years taught us that capital depletes quickly when things go bad and that there are better forms of capital to absorb loss than others. The Global Financial Crisis taught us that forward-looking capital planning is essential to ensure the success of the loss absorption properties of capital in times of financial stress.

As a Constraint

When we look at capital as a constraint, we flip the script and view it not while looking at the balance sheet as a whole, but while looking at each dollar of capital and what it supports. How does this work? Capital is literally held on a per asset basis. So, a banking organization that seeks to engage in a risky investment or loan needs to ensure that it has enough capital to support that asset. This can be a binding constraint, in that the bank may not make the investment or loan if it cannot allocate the required amount of capital to it. This is where the concept of "risk weighting" assets comes into play, such that more capital must be held against higher-risk assets and on off-balance sheet assets. As an example, with very easy math, a bank wants to buy a $1 million bond, which the capital rules assign a risk weight of 50% (so the asset is valued at $500,000—50% of $1 million).

The capital rules say the bank needs to have a ratio of 10% capital to risk-weighted assets, or $50,000 in capital, for that investment. Lawyers who represent banks in swaps, structured finance, and other complex financial instruments must be savvy with the capital treatment to ensure that capital is not indeed a binding constraint.

As a Regulatory Prerequisite

Capital is also used by the regulators as a prerequisite for many activities and expedited approvals. They liberally use being "well capitalized" as that threshold. For instance, if a banking institution seeks to help fund its activities with "brokered deposits" (deposits sourced by third parties), it must hold capital at levels considered well capitalized or seek a waiver.

As a Tool of Prudential Regulation

Much of this book addresses the need to keep banks "safe," and from that concept we have lots and lots of law that is prudential in nature—the root being "prudence." Capital serves as a valuable tool in that regard, as banking law frequently uses a percentage of capital as the maximum limit that a banking organization may engage in an activity or make an investment. For instance, a bank may loan an affiliate no more than 10% of its capital.

How Capital Impacts Bank Lawyers

As a result of what was outlined above, you can see that almost every aspect of our clients' businesses will be dependent on how much capital they hold. When we factor in the constraints and prerequisites discussed above, capital levels will determine whether they can pay dividends to shareholders; whether they can repurchase stock; whether they can accept brokered deposits; whether they can branch and merge across state lines; whether they can engage in new activities; the extent to which they can make certain investments; what kind of applications they will need to file; and their ability to make capital distributions and pay discretionary bonuses to executive officers. We also need to factor in capital calculations of lending limits, loans to insiders, affiliate transactions, and investments in certain types of instruments and subsidiaries. If our client is capital deficient, enforcement actions will ensue. If capital dissipates too much, our client will fail.

We render legal advice in connection with each of these matters. That means, in a nutshell: capital colors our world.

7

Nuts and Bolts of Prudential Law

The Necessity of "Prudence"

Banks are special. They have cheap deposit funding. Time has taught us that this "specialness" must be protected: from deposit runs, from risky activities and investments, from bad decisions, from insider and affiliate abuse. . . Thus, we have, for example, deposit insurance and access to the Federal Reserve's discount window as subsidies of enormous consequence. Many argue that their very existence validates supervision, regulation, and enforcement on the scale described in this book.

This chapter discusses four regulatory policies applicable to all depository institutions that are intended to protect them from abuse. We tend to think of these as the foundation of "prudential regulation" because they require banks to exercise "prudence." Three of these laws impose significant restrictions on banks—they must:

- limit transactions with affiliates;
- limit insider loans; and
- limit loans to one borrower.

The fourth is a policy that is expressed as a commandment: All insured depository institutions SHALL NOT operate in an unsafe and unsound manner.

Transactions with Affiliates

As long as there have been banks, they have been abused by affiliates and other insiders. Having the bank fund affiliate transactions with those cheap deposits was too great a benefit to resist. Thus, we have Sections 23A and 23B of the Federal Reserve Act (collectively, "**Sections 23A and B**"), 12 U.S.C. §§ 371c and 371c-1. They do not forbid all intra-family transactions, but they impose quantitative, qualitative, and market terms requirements on them.

Section 23A, which was enacted in 1933, originally applied to banks that were members of the Federal Reserve System (member banks). In fact, the statute still refers solely to "member banks," causing no end of confusion for young lawyers who may still decide they do not have to read it if the client is a nonmember bank or savings association. Notwithstanding the express words of the statute, it now applies, along with Section 23B, which was enacted in 1987, to federally insured nonmember banks[1] and to all savings associations[2] (referred to collectively with member banks as "banks" in this discussion).

Regulation W

The Federal Reserve has always had rulemaking authority under Sections 23A and B but declined to exercise it for decades, relying instead on staff interpretations and informal guidance. (Ever heard of "desk drawer" regulation? This practice epitomized it.) Following enactment of Gramm-Leach-Bliley, which permitted new powers to BHCs that became FHCs and, as a result, had more affiliates, the Board announced that it had saved the 23rd letter of the alphabet for this moment and it finally adopted regulations, depositing them in Regulation W, which subsumed all those historical interpretive rulings.

Regulation W is codified at 12 C.F.R. Part 223. The regulation is presented in question-and-answer format and it is often difficult to identify the proper question to find your answer. It is a good idea to read the reg through and make notes on where to find answers.

Note: It has not been updated for changes under Dodd-Frank.

Principal Restrictions

It is important to note in this regard that Sections 23A and B are all about protecting the bank from affiliate abuse. For this reason, traditional operating subsidiaries (those that can only engage in the activities of the parent bank and a few others described below) are treated as part of the protected bank—as if they were incorporated divisions.

1. In FDIA and codified at 12 U.S.C. § 1828(j).
2. In HOLA and codified at 12 U.S.C. § 1468(a).

It is useful to imagine a net around the bank and its operating subsidiaries that keeps the money from flowing to affiliates without an express exit permitted under the rules. It is also helpful to color-code the protected IDIs and the operating subsidiaries on the chart of your client's corporate family.

Section 23A protects the bank and its subsidiaries primarily from *out flows* of funds (protecting the cheap deposit base); Section 23B covers almost all transactions. The principal restrictions under Sections 23A and B may be summarized as follows:

Covered Activity	Restriction	Cite in Reg W
All "covered" transactions	Quantitative Limits:	§§ 223.11–12
	• Limited to 10% of the bank's "capital and surplus" to any single affiliate	
	• Limited to 20% of the bank's "capital and surplus" to all affiliates	
All "covered" transactions	Must be consistent with safe and sound banking practices	§ 223.13
Transfer of low-quality assets	Bank may not purchase from affiliates and sister banks	§ 223.15
Transactions with credit exposure for the bank	Must be collateralized at 100% or more	§ 223.14
All transactions (unless an exemption)	Must be on market terms	§§ 223.51–52
Attribution rule: transactions by a bank with a third party, the proceeds of which are transferred to an affiliate or that benefit an affiliate	Considered made to the affiliate	§ 223.16

If a bank has one or more affiliates and contemplates any intrafamily transactions, it is incumbent upon the board of directors to adopt a policy statement with respect to its expectations in this area, including naming the responsible parties for approvals and compliance. The policy statement, and any procedures promulgated thereunder, should not merely recite the law. They should provide direction.

More on the Quantitative Limits. As indicated above, Section 23A prohibits a bank or subsidiary from entering into a new covered transaction that (along with all other covered transactions) would exceed for that affiliate 10% of the bank's capital stock and surplus, and for all affiliates 20% of this amount. The banking agencies have promulgated identical regulations as to how capital is calculated for the purpose of prudential regulations: it is an IDI's

- Tier 1 and Tier 2 regulatory capital plus
- The ALLL not used in the bank's Tier 2 capital as of the prior Call Report.[3]

More on the Collateral Requirements. Extensions of credit to and guarantees on behalf of an affiliate (including a bank's credit exposure on derivative transactions with an affiliate and with respect to the credit exposure on borrowing or lending transactions with an affiliate) must be secured by a statutorily mandated amount of collateral. Collateral requirements range from 100% of the loan if the collateral consists of U.S. government obligations or securities of equivalent safety to 130% of the loan if the collateral is stock, leases, or other real or personal property. Debt obligations of an affiliate (as well as securities issued by an affiliate) are not permitted to be used as collateral.

Each obligation must remain secured in accordance with the collateral requirements of Section 23A *so long as it is outstanding.*

More on the Attribution Rule. Under Section 23A, a loan made to a third party for the benefit of an affiliate is regarded as a loan to the affiliate for purposes of the restrictions. A loan by the bank to a third party used to purchase an item from an affiliate of the bank, or from a company that is controlled by persons who also control the bank, is deemed to be a loan to the affiliate. Think about a control person at a bank who owns a car dealership. That person controls both the bank and the dealership. That makes the dealership an affiliate. When a customer of the bank borrows money from the bank to buy a car from the dealership—that loan is attributed to the car dealership as if it borrowed from the bank directly. Tricky thing, the attribution rule.

3. *See, e.g.*, 12 C.F.R. § 1.2(a). Capital is discussed in Chapter 6.

There are several notable exceptions to this rule, including a provision that general purpose credit cards, such as Visa- and MasterCard-branded cards, issued by a bank will be exempt from attribution if less than 25% of the purchases with the card are from an affiliate of the bank. Otherwise, if a bank issues a special purpose credit card to customers of its affiliate to purchase goods only from that affiliate, each use is under the attribution rule. (Nordstrom and other department stores operated that way for a long time when they owned credit card banks.) The preamble to the final rules points out that most banks issuing special purpose cards comply with Section 23A by selling receivables to an affiliate at the end of each day.

Definitional Challenges

Section 23A is a very short statute. In its brevity, it depends on numerous definitions. As a consequence, it can only be approached by drilling down into the definitions (some of which are italicized in the following sentence). It limits the amount of a *member bank* and its *operating subsidiary*'s *covered transactions* with a single *affiliate* to 10% of the bank's *capital stock and surplus*, and limits such transactions with all affiliates to 20% of this amount.

Term	Definition[4]
What is a Member Bank?	"Member bank" when used in the statute means any bank or savings association that has FDIC insurance or is an IDI. For example, any trust company that has FDIC insurance is a bank, but those that do not have insurance are not.
What is an Operating Subsidiary?	A company that is a subsidiary of a bank is generally considered a part of the bank within the protection of Section 23A. A subsidiary is an operating subsidiary, and not an "affiliate," *unless* it is: • a depository institution; • directly controlled by one or more affiliates of the bank (other than a depository institution affiliate) or by a shareholder or group of shareholders that control the bank; • an employee stock option plan organized for the benefit of employees, shareholders, and others related to the bank; or • a financial subsidiary, other than one operating solely as an insurance agency.[5]

4. Definitions are found in 12 C.F.R. §§ 223.2 and 223.3.
5. *See*, 12 C.F.R. § 223.3(p)(2)(i). This was a refinement added in Regulation W in deference to the fact that insurance activities did not represent principal risk, as would other activities of financial subsidiaries.

<table>
<tr>
<td>What is an Affiliate?</td>
<td>Affiliates are the entities that the bank is protected from—they are outside the "net." They are not individuals, although individuals may control the bank and also control another entity that is an affiliate because of the common control. Section 23A defines "affiliates" of banks to include the following:
• a company that controls the bank (bank holding company or savings and loan holding company);
• companies that are under common control by the bank's parent company or certain other entities, including the common control of the same individual;
• a company a majority of whose directors or general partners comprise a majority of the persons holding similar positions at the bank or the bank's parent company;
• any investment fund advised by the bank or an affiliate of the bank;
• a company in which the bank and its affiliates control more than 5% of the voting securities or equity capital of the fund;
• a depository institution that is a subsidiary of the bank;
• a partnership or LLC in which the bank or affiliate, or any officer, director, or employee thereof, serves as a general partner or managing member, respectively;
• any subsidiary of the companies described above; and
• any company, including a subsidiary of a bank, that the Federal Reserve or the primary federal regulator determines to be an affiliate by regulation or order.
Entities excluded from the definition of "affiliate" include certain companies acquired from the exercise of rights arising out of a bona fide debt previously contracted (so-called "DPC" property) and companies engaged solely in: holding the premises of the member bank; a safe deposit box business; and holding U.S. and certain U.S.-guaranteed securities.</td>
</tr>
</table>

<table>
<tr><td>What is Control?</td><td>The concept of control is a significant feature of Section 23A in order to determine which entities constitute affiliates. If an entity is not under common control or controlled by the bank, it is not an affiliate. A company or shareholder controls another company if that company or shareholder, directly or indirectly, or acting through one or more other persons:
<ul>
<li>owns, controls, or has power to vote 25% or more of any class of voting securities of the other company (including shares held by a subsidiary);</li>
<li>controls in any manner the election of a majority of the directors of the other company; or</li>
<li>is found by the Federal Reserve, after notice and opportunity for hearing, to exercise a controlling influence over the management or policies of the other company.</li>
</ul></td></tr>
<tr><td>What is a Covered Transaction?</td><td>Section 23A only applies to “covered transactions” between a bank and its operating subsidiary and an affiliate. These mostly involve funds leaving the bank. Transactions subject to the 10% and 20% quantitative limits under Section 23A include:
<ul>
<li>extensions of credit to, or purchases of assets from, an affiliate, including loans to a third party that benefit an affiliate (see discussion of attribution rules below) and including:
<ul>
<li>any transaction that creates a repayment obligation, including accidental actions that result in accounts payable to an affiliate, including paying the taxes of an affiliate or paying for services rendered on behalf of the affiliate;</li>
<li>purchase of a note or obligation of an affiliate;</li>
<li>intraday credit;</li>
<li>a purchase of assets subject to a repurchase agreement;</li>
<li>purchase of, or investment in, a security of an affiliate;</li>
</ul></li>
</ul></td></tr>
</table>

<table>
<tr><td></td><td>
<ul>
<li style="list-style-type:circle">the acceptance of a security issued by an affiliate as collateral for an extension of credit to any person or company, and the acceptance of other debt obligations of an affiliate as collateral;</li>
<li style="list-style-type:circle">the issuance of a guarantee, acceptance, or letter of credit on behalf of an affiliate, and the confirmation of a letter of credit issued by the affiliate; and</li>
<li style="list-style-type:circle">cross-affiliate netting arrangements.</li>
</ul>
<ul>
<li>a transaction with an affiliate involving the borrowing or lending of securities to the extent the transaction causes the bank to have a credit exposure to the affiliate; and</li>
<li>a derivative transaction with an affiliate to the extent that it causes the bank to have a credit exposure to the affiliate. (There is no definition yet of the term "credit exposure.")</li>
</ul>
</td></tr>
</table>

In addition, internal reorganizations and other transactions that are not specifically listed above typically involve covered transactions and, therefore, must be carefully scrutinized under the rules. For instance, the donation of a subsidiary by a parent company to a bank involves a covered transaction because the bank is deemed to have purchased the assets with an assumption of liabilities as the purchase price.[6]

Exemptions from the Provisions of Section 23A[7]

The following are the principal exemptions from the quantitative and collateral requirements of Section 23A. Each one requires adherence to the details in Regulations W:

> Transactions between a bank and a depository institution if the same company has 80% or more control of both institutions.
>
> > *This is known as the "sister bank" exemption. It is very important because it permits banks in the same corporate family to conduct routine business between them. Note, however, if both banks are not at least 80% owned then this exemption does not apply. Note also that sister banks may not sell bad assets to each other or engage in unsafe or unsound activities.*

6. 12 C.F.R. § 223.31.
7. The exemptions are in 12 C.F.R. §§ 223.41–43.

Purchase of assets from an affiliate and other transactions in connection with certain internal corporate reorganizations.

Making a loan to, or issuing a guarantee on behalf of, an affiliate *that is fully secured by U.S. obligations or a segregated, earmarked deposit account* at the bank.

> *This exemption is particularly useful, permitting an affiliate to convey control of a securities account or deposit account to the bank sufficient in amount to collateralize any covered transaction. That takes the transaction out of Section 23A, so it is a big deal.*

Purchasing an extension of credit from an affiliate on a nonrecourse basis subject to certain limits, including the following: (i) the bank must make an independent evaluation of the borrower's creditworthiness before the loan is made, and (ii) the bank may not purchase each year more than 50% of the loans originated by the affiliate (historically called the "250.250 exception" because of its previous citation as an official interpretation at 12 C.F.R. § 250.250).

Purchasing a security from a securities affiliate of the member bank if the bank or the securities affiliate is acting exclusively as a riskless principal, and the security purchased is not issued, underwritten, or sold as principal (other than as riskless principal) by any affiliate of the member bank.

Purchasing from an affiliate a loan originated by the bank and sold to the affiliate subject to a repurchase agreement or with recourse.

Extensions of intraday credit to an affiliate, if the bank maintains policies and procedures reasonably designed to manage the credit exposure of these transactions, the transactions comply with the "arm's length" requirements of Section 23B, and the bank ceases to treat the transaction as an extension of intraday credit at the end of the bank's business day in the United States.

"Super 23A"

A 23A wrinkle was introduced as part of the Volcker Rule's prohibition on investments in covered funds. In the so-called "Super 23A" provision, outright prohibitions are imposed on certain transactions between banking entities and covered funds that they sponsor or advise—extensions of credit, guarantees issued on behalf of the fund, and purchases of assets or securities from the fund. There has been a lingering question as to whether typical Section 23A exemptions, described above, would apply. In the banking agencies' 2019 final rule on Volcker,[8] they clarified that the historical Section 23A exemptions apply, and they provided an additional exemption for an extension of credit to, or purchase of asset from, a covered fund, as long as:

The transaction is in the ordinary course of business in connection with payment transactions, settlement services, or futures, derivatives, and securities clearing;
Each extension of credit is repaid, sold, or terminated by the end of five business day; and
The banking entity making each extension of credit has established and maintains policies and procedures reasonably designed to manage the credit exposure arising from the extension of credit in a safe and sound manner and ensure that it is on market terms and has no reason to believe that the covered fund will have difficulty repaying the extension of credit in accordance with its terms.

Basic Provisions of Section 23B

Section 23B was added to assure that affiliates did not have sweetheart deals with banks and their subsidiaries. As a result, it sweeps more broadly in terms of the transactions that it covers. For purposes of Section 23B, the terms "subsidiary" and "affiliate" have the same meaning as in Section 23A, except the term "affiliate" does not include an insured depository institution.

Market Terms Requirement. Section 23B requires that certain transactions between a bank and its affiliates be on "market terms," that is, on terms including credit standards that are prevailing at the time for comparable transactions, or in the absence of comparable transactions, on terms that in good faith would be offered to nonaffiliated companies. This means that banks must either find comparables for the transaction or validate that the terms would be offered to unaffiliated parties. It also means that banks and their affiliates need to have arms-length, negotiated contracts in place for the transactions to which Section 23B applies.

The market terms requirement applies to:

- all transactions that are "covered transactions" under Section 23A and has the same exemptions; and
- the following transactions that are not "covered transactions" under Section 23A:

8. Prohibitions and Restrictions on Proprietary Trading and Certain Interests in, and Relationships With, Hedge Funds and Private Equity Funds, 84 Fed. Reg. 61,974 (Nov. 14, 2019).

Payments of money or furnishing services to an affiliate
Transactions in which an affiliate acts as an agent or broker or receives a fee for its services to the bank or to any other person
Transactions with a third party if an affiliate has a financial interest in the third party or is a participant in the transaction (like the Attribution Rule under 23A)

Prohibited Asset Purchases.[9] A bank or its subsidiary may not purchase as fiduciary any securities (as defined in Section 3(a)(10) of the Securities Exchange Act of 1934[10]) from an affiliate unless the purchase is permitted: (i) under the instrument creating the fiduciary relationship, (ii) by court order, or (iii) by the law of the jurisdiction governing the fiduciary relationship.

Banks either acting as principal or fiduciary are also prohibited from purchasing or otherwise acquiring any security during the existence of any underwriting or selling syndicate, if a principal underwriter of that security is an affiliate of such bank, unless: (i) the purchase was approved, before the securities were initially offered for sale to the public, by a majority of the directors of the bank; and (ii) the approval was based on a determination that the purchase is a sound investment for the bank, irrespective of the fact that an affiliate of the bank is the principal underwriter.

Advertising Rule.[11] A bank or any subsidiary or affiliate of a bank may not publish any advertisement or enter into any agreement stating or suggesting that the bank will in any way be responsible for the obligations of its affiliates. This provision, however, does not prohibit a bank from issuing a guarantee, acceptance, or letter of credit on behalf of an affiliate, confirming a letter of credit, or entering into a cross-affiliate netting arrangement, to the extent that the transaction satisfies the quantitative limits and collateral requirements of Section 23A.

Section 23A and B Examples

The application of Sections 23A and B to several simple transactions between a bank and another member of the bank holding company family is provided below.

9. 12 C.F.R. § 223.53.
10. 15 U.S.C. Section 78c(a)(10).
11. 12 C.F.R. § 223.54.

Loan to a Holding Company Subsidiary	If a subsidiary bank makes a loan to a holding company subsidiary, this transaction will fall within the category of "covered transactions." As a covered transaction, the bank would be subject to the quantitative limitations of Section 23A and the applicable restrictions of Section 23B. Further, since the loan is an extension of credit to an affiliate requiring collateral security, the transaction will be subject to the collateral requirements of Section 23A.
Holding Company Stock as Collateral for Bank Loan	If a customer of a subsidiary bank offers stock of the holding company to secure a loan from the subsidiary bank, this transaction will also fall within the category of "covered transactions." Because this transaction does not create a repayment obligation of an affiliate, the bank will not be subject to the collateral requirements of Section 23A but will be subject to the quantitative limitations of Section 23A and the applicable restrictions of Section 23B. The affiliate for these purposes is the issuer of the stock—the holding company.
Bank Lease of Property from Holding Company	If a subsidiary bank leases property from a holding company, this transaction will not fall within the definition of "covered transactions," and the bank will not be subject to the limitations or requirements of Section 23A. However, as this transaction is one of the specified transactions under Section 23B, the lease must be on comparable terms as leases offered to nonaffiliates and it must comply with the other applicable restrictions of Section 23B.
Bank Loan of Operating Funds to Its Insurance Agency Subsidiary	A nonbank subsidiary of a bank engaged in insurance sales is excluded from the definition of "affiliate" by Regulation Y, even if it is a financial subsidiary otherwise. Therefore, neither the quantitative nor qualitative restrictions of Section 23A nor the additional restrictions of Section 23B would apply to a bank loan to its nonbank subsidiary.

Insider Loans

Speaking of abuse, insiders were even more guilty than affiliates of taking sweetheart deals, prompting Congress to enact Sections 22(g) and 22(h) of the FRA, 12 U.S.C. §§ 375a and 375b. The rules were deposited in the FRA, like Section 23A and B, because they originally only applied to member banks subject to Federal Reserve supervision. As it did with the provisions on transactions with affiliates, Congress extended the sections on insider loans to state nonmember banks and savings associations over time.[12]

These provisions impose restrictions on extensions of credit that a bank may make to the bank's directors, executive officers, and principal stockholders and also apply, with certain exceptions, to persons who hold these insider positions in the bank's affiliates.[13] Subsidiaries of banks are considered part of the bank itself under this law, as with Sections 23A and B. As a result, extensions of credit by bank subsidiaries to the bank's insiders are counted as loans made by the bank for purposes of the insider lending restrictions.

Regulation O

The Federal Reserve's insider loan rules are implemented by Regulation O. Regulation O also applies to credit card banks, ILCs, and certain other institutions that are excluded from the definition of "bank" under the BHCA and to the companies that control these institutions.[14]

Regulation O is codified at 12 C.F.R. Part 215.

Insiders Subject to Regulation O

Regulation O applies to insiders, which are defined with the following permutations:

---

12. These rules are applied to state nonmember banks by 12 U.S.C. § 1828(j). Section 22(h) of the FRA, which deals with loans to all insiders and executive officers, was applied to state nonmember banks in 1978 by Section 108 of Pub. Law 95-630 (Nov. 10, 1978), 92 Stat. 3664. Section 22(g), relating to loans to executive officers, was added in Section 18(j) in 1991. Insider loan rules are applied to savings associations by Section 11(b) of the Home Owners' Loan Act (HOLA) (12 U.S.C. § 1468(b)). Section 22(h) of the FRA was applied to savings associations by Section 301 of FIRREA. Regulation O now applies to savings associations. *See*, 12 C.F.R. § 163.43.
13. Affiliates include any parent company of the bank and any subsidiary of the parent company that represents 10% or more of the consolidated assets of the parent company.
14. Subsidiaries of a parent company that represent 10% or less of the consolidated assets of the parent company are generally excluded from coverage under Regulation O.

Term	Definition
What is an Insider?[14]	Directors, executive officers, and principal shareholders. Regulation O imposes limits not only on extensions of credit that the bank may make to its own insiders but also, with some exceptions, on extensions of credit to persons who are insiders of the bank's subsidiaries, parent company, if any, and certain subsidiaries of the parent company.
What is a Director?	This term is given its normal meaning; Regulation O provides that a person's status as a director is not dependent on the person receiving compensation for his or her service. Advisory directors who are unelected, who do not vote and are not authorized to vote on matters before the board of directors, and who provide solely general policy advice are not "directors" for purposes of Regulation O.
What is an Executive Officer?	Executive officers of a company or bank are persons who participate or have authority to participate (other than in the capacity of a director) in major policymaking functions of the company or bank regardless of their title. It should be noted, however, that there are certain officer positions that are presumed under Regulation O to be executive officer positions, including: • chairperson of the board; • president; • vice president; • secretary; • treasurer; or • cashier. The above-mentioned officers will be considered "executive officers" for purposes of Regulation O, *unless* (i) the officer is excluded by resolution of the board of directors or by the bylaws of the entity from participating (other than as a director) in major policymaking functions of the entity; and (ii) the person does not in fact participate in them. There tends to be a heavy regulatory presumption against excluding certain officers from the designation of executive officer, including: (i) any officer whose title contains the word "Chief;" and (ii) the chairperson of the board.

14. Subsidiaries of a parent company that represent 10% or less of the consolidated assets of the parent company are generally excluded from coverage under Regulation O.

What is a Principal Shareholder?	These are persons other than banks (and any company that controls the bank) that, directly or indirectly, or "acting through or in concert with others," own or control the power to vote more than 10% of any class of voting shares of a bank or company. For purposes of determining whether an individual is a principal shareholder for purposes of Regulation O, shares owned or controlled by a member of a person's "immediate family" are considered to be held by that person. "Immediate family" is defined in Regulation O to include the spouse of an individual, the individual's minor children, and any of the individual's children (including adults) residing in the individual's home.
What is a Related Interest?	Regulation O covers extensions of credit to insiders and to their "related interests." These are businesses and other companies controlled by the insider and political or campaign committees that are controlled by an insider or that provide funds or services that benefit the insider. Regulation O establishes a conclusive presumption of control triggered when a person, directly or indirectly, or acting through or in concert with others: (i) owns, controls, or has the power to vote 25% or more of a class of the voting securities of an entity; (ii) controls in any manner over the election of a majority of the directors of the company; or (iii) has the ability to exercise a controlling influence over the management or policies of the company (regardless of the individual's percentage ownership interest in the company). Regulation O establishes rebuttable presumption of control triggered when a person, directly or indirectly, or *acting in concert* with others, owns, controls, or has the power to vote more than 10% and less than 25% of any class of the company's voting securities if the individual either: (i) is an executive officer or director of the company; or (ii) is the company's single largest holder of the company's voting securities.

Principal Provisions of Regulation O

Loan Limits. "Extensions of credit" to insiders are subject to certain "loan limits":

What is an Extension of Credit?	Broadly defined under Regulation O to include virtually any transaction as a result of which a person becomes obligated to pay money or its equivalent to a bank. This includes not only loans and lines of credit, but also certain advances of unearned salary, overdraft advances,[15] certain standby letters of credit, and more. Moreover, the term includes credit exposure to a person from a derivative transaction, repurchase agreement, reverse repurchase agreement, securities lending transaction, or securities borrowing transaction.
What is the Loan Limit?	There are four sets of overlapping loan limits in Regulation O: • loans to all insiders that require prior board approval; • separate rules on loans to executive officers of the bank; • a ceiling on the aggregate amount of loans that a bank may have outstanding to all insiders at any one time; and • a limit on the maximum amount of loans that may be outstanding to a single borrower.

Loans to insiders of the bank, its subsidiaries, and certain affiliates (except loans to executive officers of the bank) and loans to the related interests of those insiders, require prior approval of a majority of the entire bank's board of directors (with any interested director recusing themselves from discussion and abstaining from the vote) if, when combined with all other outstanding loans from the bank to that person and the person's related interests, they would exceed either: the greater of $25,000 or 5% of the bank's unimpaired capital and unimpaired surplus;[16] or $500,000. Prior board approval is not required if the loan is made pursuant to a line of credit approved by the board within 14 months of the loan.

15. Overdraft advances by executive officers and directors of a bank are subject to separate and distinct restrictions set forth in 12 C.F.R. § 215.4(e).

16. A bank's unimpaired capital and unimpaired surplus equals the bank's Tier 1 and Tier 2 capital plus the balance of the bank's allowance for loan and lease losses not included in its Tier 2 capital for regulatory reporting purposes.

Bank Executive Officer "Carve Out." Separate rules apply to extensions of credit to executive officers of the bank. These rules permit the following extensions of credit, subject to the bank's normal underwriting standards:

Loans "in any amount"	for financing, subject to certain restrictions, the purchase, construction, or rehabilitation of their principal residence, for education of their children, and loans secured by certain interests in securities or by a segregated account. The phrase "in any amount" in Regulation O means that the loans can be for any amount up to the loans to one borrower limit summarized below, if the loan is made on a non-preferential basis and the executive officer meets the bank's underwriting standards for the loan.
Loans for "other purposes"	which may not exceed at any one time the higher of 2.5% of the bank's unimpaired capital and unimpaired surplus or $25,000, but in no event more than $100,000.

Maximum Loan to One Borrower. Regulation O provides that the maximum extension of credit that may be outstanding by a member bank to any one insider and his or her related interests is the loans to one borrower limit that is applied to national banks by Section 5200 of the Revised Statutes (remember – national banks must be member banks). As discussed below, this limit is:

- 15% of the bank's unimpaired capital and surplus for extensions of credit not fully secured; plus
- an additional 10% of the bank's unimpaired capital and unimpaired surplus in the case of extensions of credit that are fully secured by readily marketable collateral.

For state banks chartered in a state that has a lending limit lower than that provided in Section 5200, the lower rate will prevail. Additional requirements and restrictions apply to overdrafts of directors and executive officers of member banks.[17]

Aggregate Loan Limit. Section 22(h) provides that, subject to certain exceptions, the aggregate amount of extensions of credit outstanding to all insiders may not exceed the bank's unimpaired capital and unimpaired surplus.[18] Banks with deposits of less than $100 million that are well managed

17. 12 C.F.R. § 215.4(e).

18. *Id. See also,* 12 C.F.R. § 215.4(d).

and well capitalized may have up to twice that amount if authorized by an annual resolution of the bank's board of directors, which must determine, among other things, that the higher limit is consistent with safe and sound banking practices.

In addition to the quantitative restrictions on extensions of credit to insiders described above, Regulation O also imposes qualitative requirements on insider loans. Regulation O requires that an extension of credit:

- be made on substantially the same terms as, and following underwriting standards that are no less stringent than, those prevailing at the time for comparable transactions with non-insiders; and
- does not involve more than the normal risk of repayment or present other unfavorable features.

Recordkeeping Requirements

Recordkeeping for Insiders of the Bank. Regulation O requires banks to adopt recordkeeping methods that:

- identify, through an annual survey, all insiders of the bank; and
- maintain records of all extensions of credit to insiders of the bank itself, including the amount and terms of each such extension of credit.[19]

Recordkeeping for Insiders of Affiliates. Regulation O had also required banks to identify all directors, officers, and principal shareholders of the bank and its affiliates (and their related interests) and to specify the amounts and terms of all credit extended to these insiders. By the time the Federal Reserve Board considered adoption of amendments to Regulation O in 1994, it was obvious that financial institution holding companies had become so large and widely dispersed that literal compliance with these requirements was not practical. The Federal Reserve realized that large banking organizations with "hundreds of affiliates with thousands of officers and directors would have no practical way to know who they are or whether they have a loan with the bank"[20] and adopted an amendment to Regulation O permitting banks to use one of the three following methods to make these reports:[21]

19. 12 C.F.R. § 215.8(b).

20. Staff memo presented Jan. 24, 1994, during meeting at which the Board adopted final regulations amending Regulation O at 56 Fed. Reg. 8,837 (Feb. 24, 1994).

21. 12 C.F.R. § 215.8(c).

Survey method	Identifying each insider of the bank's affiliates through an annual survey and keeping records of extensions of credit made to these insiders;
Borrower inquiry method	Requiring as part of each extension of credit that the borrower indicate whether the borrower is an insider of an affiliate of the bank, and maintaining records that identify the amount and terms of each extension of credit by the bank to borrowers so identifying themselves; or
Alternative recordkeeping method	As approved by the bank's principal federal regulator.

Other Reports. Upon receipt of a written request from a member of the public, a bank must disclose the names of its executive officers and principal shareholders who, along with their related interests, received extensions of credit from the bank as of the latest previous quarter of the year, that in the aggregate equaled or exceeded 5% of the bank's capital and unimpaired surplus or $500,000, whichever amount is less.[22] Additionally, each executive officer or director of a bank that is not publicly traded must report annually to the board of directors the outstanding amount of any extension of credit that is secured by the stock of the bank.[23]

Purchases of Assets from Insiders

Section 615 of Dodd-Frank extends the protections afforded by Regulation O by adding a section prohibiting a bank from purchasing an asset from an "insider" unless: the transaction is on market terms; and, if it represents more than 10% of the capital of the bank, it is approved in advance by a majority of the disinterested members of the board of directors.[24]

Loans to One Borrower

The oldest form of prudential regulation governs how much a bank may lend to one borrower. The "lending limit" or "loans to one borrower" (**LTOB**) limit is intended to assure that no concentration of credit exists such that one borrower could cause the failure of the bank. It also promotes diversification of the loan portfolio.

22. 12 C.F.R. § 215.9(b).
23, 12 C.F.R. § 215.10.
24. *Amending* Section 18 of the FDIA (12 U.S.C. § 2828) by adding a subsection (z).

> *Note: the banking agencies also supervise concentrations at banks, and that is different from LTOB. A concentration could be numerous loans to one industry or in one segment (e.g., commercial loans) and the agencies have issued various guidelines, usually under the rubric of safety and soundness, with respect to concentrations of credit.*

Specific LTOB Limits by Charter

National Banks and Federal Thrifts. The lending limit for national banks is codified at 12 U.S.C. § 84, with the OCC regulations at 12 C.F.R. Part 32. The OCC published an Interim Final Rule on June 21, 2012,[25] in order to amend its regulation to consolidate the lending limit rules applicable to national banks and savings associations and remove its separate regulation governing lending limits for savings associations. Thus, the OCC rules apply to federal savings associations from July 21, 2012, forward.

The lending limit for national banks and federal savings associations is:

Unsecured Limit	15% of the institution's capital and surplus (defined in the same manner as for Regulation W and Regulation O).
Secured Limit	plus an additional 10% of the institution's capital and surplus if the loan is fully secured by readily marketable collateral (together with the unsecured portion, the "general lending limit"). Readily marketable collateral is narrowly defined to include financial instruments (securities traded on a national exchange, commercial paper, negotiated certificates of deposit, and shares of mutual funds) and bullion that are salable under ordinary market conditions with reasonable promptness at a fair value determined by quotations based on actual transactions at an auction or similarly available daily bid and ask price markets.
Corporate Group Limit	not to exceed, in the aggregate, 50% of the lending bank's capital and surplus. This 50% limitation applies even if loans to some or all of the members of the corporate group are not required to be combined for purposes of the general lending limit. OCC regulations define a corporate group as consisting of a person or entity and all other entities in which such person or entity owns 50% or more of the voting securities or voting interests.

25. 77 Fed. Reg. 37,265 (June 21, 2012).

State Banks. State banks and state savings associations are subject to similar provisions under state law, although they tend to be less stringent.

Disparity Relief. OCC regulations include provisions that address, in part, this lending limit disparity between national banks and state-chartered banks in states that have higher lending limits than national banks. Under the OCC lending limit regulations,[26] an eligible national bank is able (subject to receipt of prior OCC approval) to increase its lending limit with respect to one- to four-family residential real estate loans, loans to small businesses, and certain agricultural loans by an amount equal to the lesser of (i) 10% of its capital and surplus or (ii) the percent of its capital and surplus, in excess of 15%, that a state-chartered bank is permitted to lend under the applicable laws of the state in which the national bank's main office is located (the "increased lending limits"). A national bank's outstanding loans to any one borrower made under the increased lending limits, when aggregated with loans made to the same borrower under the OCC's general lending limit, may not exceed 25% of the lending bank's capital and surplus. Further, a national bank's total outstanding loans to all borrowers made under the increased lending limits may not exceed 100% of the bank's capital and surplus.

Extensions of Credit

Lending limits apply to a vast assortment of transactions defined generally as "loans or extensions of credit":[27]

A contractual commitment to advance funds
Purchase of securities subject to repurchase; exception for government securities where a bank has assured control over the collateral
Purchase of third-party paper subject to repurchase
Overdrafts, whether prearranged or not, but not intraday
Charged-off loans, unless unenforceable
Fed funds sold with a maturity of more than one day
A guarantee fund and initial margin to a clearing house

The OCC also includes credit exposures arising from derivative transactions, repurchase agreements, reverse repurchase agreements, securities lending transactions, and securities borrowing transactions.

The following are NOT loans or extensions of credit:[28]

Additional advances for taxes, insurance, utilities to preserve the value of the collateral of the bank

26. 12 C.F.R. § 32.7.
27. 12 C.F.R. § 32.2(k)(1).
28. 12 C.F.R. § 32.2(k)(2).

The financed sale of a bank's own assets
Accrued interest
Renewal or restructured loans if no new money extended or no new borrower
A nonrecourse participation where credit risk is shared
Commercial letters of credit, not standby or commitments

In addition, there are numerous exceptions, including:

- loans secured by U.S. obligations or those guaranteed by a federal agency
- loans to or guaranteed by the general obligations of a state or political subdivision loans secured by segregated deposit accounts
- loans secured by discount of commercial paper
- 35% limit for loans secured by bills of lading or warehouse receipts covering readily marketable staples
- loans participated without recourse to the originating bank—do not count the number of participations.

Attribution Rules

What makes lending limit law more difficult is that "one borrower" is much broader in practice than one individual or one company. Section 84(d)(2) provides authority to the OCC to determine when a loan putatively made to one person will be attributable to another person. The regulations of the OCC at 12 C.F.R. § 32.5 require a loan to a named borrower to be attributed to the other borrower(s) under a direct benefit test and a common enterprise test.

This is a highly important and risky analysis. Lawyers should exercise caution in passing on any loan under LTOB without a thorough examination of the facts and relationships. Lawyers have been the subject of enforcement orders and fines in this regard.

In summary, the guidance is:

If the named borrower is a partnership, joint venture, or association, the loan will be attributed to the partners or members of the entity unless:

- the agreement establishing the partnership, joint venture, or association provides that the members of the entity are not personally liable for the obligations of the entity; and
- those provisions of the agreement are valid under applicable law.

A loan to a named borrower will be attributed to the other borrower(s) if:

- the proceeds of the loan, or assets purchased with loan proceeds, are transferred to the other borrower(s), other than in a bona fide arm's-length transaction where the proceeds are used to acquire goods, property, or services; or
- a common enterprise exists between the named borrower and the other borrower(s).

A "**common enterprise**" will be found to exist if:

- the expected source of repayment for loans made to both the named borrower and the other borrower(s) are the same and no borrower has another source of income from which the loan and the borrower's other obligations can be repaid;
- the named borrower and the other borrower(s) are related through common control and there is substantial financial interdependence between the borrowers;[29]
- the named borrower and the other borrower(s) use the loan proceeds to acquire more than 50% of a business enterprise, without regard to whether each borrower is otherwise creditworthy independently of either the business enterprise or the other borrower(s); or
- the OCC determines that a common enterprise exists, based on the facts and circumstances of a particular transaction.

Factors that have been considered by the OCC in making such a determination include whether the borrowers: (i) engage in supporting lines of business; (ii) interchange goods and services; (iii) share common ownership of assets, common management, or use of common facilities; (iv) commingle assets and liabilities; (v) engage in closely related business activities; (vi) have similar structures, financing, and holdings; (vii) may receive financial aid from each other; (viii) are members of the same family; and (ix) pledge assets to support another's loans.

National banks would generally be required to combine loans to separate borrowers when the source of repayment for the loans is the same, the creditworthiness of the named borrower would not justify the loan without reliance on the creditworthiness of the other borrower(s), or the primary beneficiary of the loan was the other borrower(s), rather than the named borrower.

29. "Substantial financial interdependence" is deemed to exist if 50% or more of the annual gross receipts or gross expenditures of one borrower are derived from transactions with another person or entity.

Noncompliant and Nonconforming Loans

When a bank makes a loan that is "**overline**," *i.e.*, over the lending limit when it is made, *the board of directors is deemed to be personally responsible for the loan until the last penny is paid.*[30] That is pretty sobering news to any client and is a very effective prophylactic to assure compliance.

Loans are deemed nonconforming if they later exceed the lending limit. No remedy is required during the term of the loan if the loan complied with limits when made. However, if the collateral value declines, the borrower must post more collateral within 30 days. Additionally, before a bank can renew a nonconforming loan, it must make a good faith effort to bring the loan back into compliance with the lending limit.

Interplay among Prudential Regulations

There are numerous situations in which a given loan may be subject to the lending limit, as well as Regulation W and/or Regulation O. In addition, a bank may buy debt of a customer that is subject to different rules under investment limitations in 12 U.S.C. § 24 (Seventh) and 12 C.F.R. Part 1. How are these reconciled? According to the OCC, the lending limit does not apply to covered transactions with affiliates; it does apply to Regulation O loans; and the investment limits provide additional leeway, such that a bank may invest in debt up to the limit in Section 24 (Seventh) and 12 C.F.R. Part 1 (10%) and further loan that borrower up to the lending limit.[31]

Safety and Soundness

Prudential regulation, like that described above, targets forms of abuse. Noncompliance constitutes a violation of law and is punishable by the regulators. But, there are so many other actions that may cause harm or put the stability of a bank at risk, but that are not the subject of a legal prohibition, such as underwriting loans, asset growth, concentrations of credit, consumer services, interest rate exposure, brokered deposits, new products, compensation practices, and so on. You can see the need for a backstop that captures all the harmful practices not identified in other laws. That backstop is a concept called "safety and soundness," applied bank by bank and on a macro level (to the industry as a whole). The failure of an institution to manage to safety and soundness standards manifests in "unsafe and unsound" banking practices.

---

30. del Junco v. Conover, *aff'd*, 682 F2d 1338 (9th Cir. 1982). This policy has now been codified in the FDIA, permitting the banking agencies to seek restitution from directors for violations of law. *See*, 12 U.S.C. § 1818(b)(6).

31. 12 C.F.R. § 32.1(c)(1)-(3).

Unsafe and Unsound Banking Practices

Unsafe and unsound banking practices, along with violations of law and breaches of fiduciary duty, define bad bank behavior and serve as the predicate for regulatory criticism and enforcement.[32] That means when safety and soundness is at issue, a bank and its affiliated persons may be punished for engaging in a pattern or practice that is not *per se* illegal.

Yet, given its importance, and despite the fact that the FDIA and other federal banking laws sprinkle the concept of engaging in unsafe and unsound practices liberally, Congress has not defined the term, leaving it to the regulators and the courts. To that end, the OCC suggests that unsafe and unsound banking practices "encompass ... conduct deemed contrary to accepted standards of banking operations which might result in abnormal risk or loss to a banking institution or shareholder."[33] Courts point out that this is a fact-based inquiry:

> What constitutes an unsafe and unsound condition is somewhat of an amorphous concept, as it varies depending on the circumstances involved. It is clear, however, that an unsafe or unsound condition exists where a financial institution is operated in such a manner as to cause unacceptable levels of risk to its depositors' funds. Since a particular condition may not necessarily be unsafe or unsound in every circumstance, it must be judged in relation to all relevant facts.[34]

"Amorphous concept"?? "Varies depending on the circumstances"!! What this all boils down to is that "safety and soundness" serves as the regulatory predicate to make behavior subject to penalty that is not otherwise a violation of law and is subjective in application. It may be the ultimate "gotcha" in our business.

Regulatory Context

Notwithstanding, the federal banking agencies have provided context by adopting interagency rules that establish operational and managerial standards to promote the safety and soundness of federally insured depository

32. *See,* 12 U.S.C § 1818, where each of these three misbehaviors triggers various enforcement actions.

33. Sinclair v. Hawke, 314 F.3d 934 n. 2 (2003), citing First Nat'l Bank of Eden v. Dept. of the Treasury, 568 F.2d 610, 611 n. 2 (8th Cir.1978). See also, Michael v. F.D.I.C., 687 F.3d 337 (2012) and Doolittle v. National Credit Union Ass'n, 992 F.2d 1531 (1993).

34. Franklin Sav. Ass'n v. Director, Office of Thrift Supervision, 934 F.2d 1127 (1991)

institutions.[35] The rules include the following noteworthy interagency appendices:

Appendix	Coverage
Appendix A	Covers standards for internal controls, information systems, internal audit systems, loan documentation, credit underwriting, interest rate exposure, asset growth, excessive compensation, fees and benefits, asset quality, and earnings.
Appendix B	Includes the *Interagency Guidelines Establishing Information Security Systems*, the rules banks must follow to assure that they and their vendors protect customer information under the requirements of the Gramm-Leach-Bliley Act.
Appendix C	Includes the *Guidelines Establishing Standards for Residential Mortgage Practices.*
Appendix D	Where the regulators deposited the heightened standards for risk management in large institutions.

Risk Management

The definitions of unsafe and unsound banking practices set forth above each emphasize the existence of "abnormal risk" and "unacceptable levels of risk." From the perspective of the bank regulatory agencies, the failure of an insured depository institution to provide effective risk management constitutes an unsafe and unsound banking practice. While we cannot de-risk banking, we can manage it. Thus, from the foundation of safety and soundness springs the construct of risk management—perhaps the most important commandment in the regulatory lexicon of the early 21st century.

During the past decade, the bank regulatory agencies have increasingly emphasized the importance of sound risk management processes and strong internal controls when evaluating the activities of the IDIs they supervise. Properly managing risk has been identified as critical to the conduct of safe and sound banking activities and has become even more important as new technologies, product innovation, and the size and speed of financial transactions have changed the nature

35. (OCC) 12 C.F.R. § 30; (Federal Reserve) 12 C.F.R. § 208 (Regulation H), Appendix D-1 and D-2; (FDIC) 12 C.F.R. § 364. The FDIC also has promulgated regulations at Part 337 that address unsafe and unsound banking practices in connection with other areas, including letters of credit and brokered deposits.

of banking markets. The agencies have identified a spectrum of risks facing a banking institution including, but not limited to, credit, market, liquidity, operational, legal, and reputational risk.

Bank regulators identify key risk themes each year, including, for example: credit risk management and commercial and residential real estate concentration risk management; vendor management, incentive compensation practices, AML compliance, cybersecurity, and CRA performance. Banks are expected to have active board and senior management oversight; adequate policies, procedures and limits; adequate risk measurement, monitoring and management information systems; and comprehensive internal controls.

Enforcement

How do we police safety and soundness and risk management? Federal law provides a waterfall of potential regulatory reaction to unsafe and unsound practices, depending on the severity of the misbehavior. If an agency identifies an unsafe and unsound banking practice, it may start more informally and require the bank to submit a plan for achieving and maintaining compliance. If a bank fails to submit an acceptable compliance plan, or fails in any material respect to implement a compliance plan that has been accepted by its primary federal regulator, the regulator is required to issue an order directing the bank to cure the deficiency. Until the deficiency cited in the regulator's order is cured, the regulator may restrict the bank's rate 1of growth, require the bank to increase its capital, restrict the rates the bank pays on deposits, or require the bank to take any action the regulator deems appropriate under the circumstances.

Noncompliance with safety and soundness may also constitute grounds for cease-and-desist orders and civil money penalty assessments, as discussed in Chapter 8, or even bank failure.

8

Fundamentals of Bank Examination and Enforcement

This chapter was originally authored by John M. Geiringer and Stanley F. Orszula, Barack Ferrazzano Financial Institutions Group

Policing Depository Institutions

Who can forget the "flinty-eyed" examiner—Mr. Carter—who almost cost Jimmy Stewart his building and loan association in *It's a Wonderful Life*? (If you don't understand that reference, watch the movie at your earliest convenience—it's required viewing for every bank regulatory lawyer!)

Critical components of the protection of our banking system are the supervisory and enforcement roles of the bank regulators, who send in troops of examiners to evaluate compliance with the law and safety and soundness concerns, armed with an arsenal of examination manuals and checklists.

> *Examination manuals are one of the best sources of informal guidance on every banking subject imagined by the regulators. They are housed on the various regulatory websites listed at the end of chapter 2, and many are on the Federal Financial Institutions Examination Council (**FFIEC**) website.*
> *On that note, it is important to know that the FFIEC is an interagency body composed of the bank regulatory agencies and empowered to prescribe uniform principles, standards, and reporting forms for the federal supervision and examination of financial institutions. See, http://www.ffiec.gov.*

Bank Holding Company and Savings and Loan Holding Company Inspections

The Federal Reserve, through its constituent Federal Reserve Banks, conducts inspections of BHCs and THCs under similar processes. Holding company inspection (as the Federal Reserve calls it) is unique because the Federal Reserve is required to cooperate with the other banking regulators.[1] The Federal Reserve is also charged with examining nonbanking subsidiaries of the holding companies.[2] The primary inspections are to determine the overall enterprise's financial condition and whether the entity is complying with its applicable laws and regulations; while bank-level examinations are generally comprised of safety and soundness, compliance, and other specialty examinations.

Systemically Important and Large BHCs/THCs

In the wake of the 2008 Global Financial Crisis, the Federal Reserve became responsible for enterprise-wide supervision of those holding companies that pose risks to the U.S. financial system.[3] The Federal Reserve uses a large financial institution (**LFI**) rating system for systemically important BHCs, and for BHCs and noninsurance THCs with greater than $100 billion in total consolidated assets. The largest holding companies and banks have resident examiners permanently stationed on-site.

LFI Rating System.

Read about the LFI at https://www.federalreserve.gov/supervisionreg/srletters/sr1903.htm.

The LFI rating system has three components:

Component	Coverage
Capital Planning and Positions	This component measures "(i) the effectiveness of a firm's governance and planning processes used to determine the amount of capital necessary to cover risks and exposures, and to support activities through a range of conditions and events; and (ii) the sufficiency of a firm's capital positions to comply with applicable regulatory requirements and to support the firm's ability to continue to serve as a financial intermediary through a range of conditions."

1. 12 C.F.R. § 225.5(c).
2. 12 U.S.C. § 5361(b).
3. 12 U.S.C. § 5365(a).

Liquidity Risk Management and Positions	This component evaluates "(i) the effectiveness of a firm's governance and risk management processes used to determine the amount of liquidity necessary to cover risks and exposures, and to support activities through a range of conditions; and (ii) the sufficiency of a firm's liquidity positions to comply with applicable regulatory requirements and to support the firm's ongoing obligations through a range of conditions."
Governance and Controls	This final metric "assesses a firm's effectiveness in aligning strategic business objectives with the firm's risk appetite and risk management capabilities; maintaining effective and independent risk management and control functions, including internal audit; promoting compliance with laws and regulations, including those related to consumer protection; and otherwise planning for the ongoing resiliency of the firm." Additional focus is placed on the board of directors, management of business lines, independent risk management, and with respect to a limited number of U.S. holding companies subject to the Federal Reserve's Large Institution Supervision Coordinating Committee Framework, recovery planning.

Each of the foregoing factors is rated on the following descending scale: Broadly Meets Expectations, Conditionally Meets Expectations, Deficient-1, and Deficient-2.

Other BHCs/THCs

All other non-LFI holding companies are rated differently under the Federal Reserve's **RFI/C(D)** rating system (not an easy acronym to pronounce), comprised of: **R**isk, **F**inancial condition, potential **I**mpact of the holding company, and other non-bank subsidiaries on the bank, **C**omposite rating, and **D**epository institution.

> *Read about the RFI/C(D) at*
> *https://www.federalreserve.gov/supervisionreg/srletters/sr1321.htm.*

The RFI/C(D) Rating System. Each component of the RFI/C(D) rating is also based on a "1" to "5" scale, and some components may be given more weight than others depending on the holding company's size, complexity of operations, and risk profile. A rating of "1" indicates superior condition and a rating of "5" shows grave concern by the Federal Reserve. The coverage of the components of the RFI/C(D) rating system are:

Component	Coverage
Risk	The holding company's ability to manage risk, including board and management oversight, policies and procedures, risk monitoring, and internal controls.
Financial Condition	The overall financial condition of the holding company, which includes capital, earnings, liquidity, and asset quality.
Impact	Whether the holding company could adversely affect the subsidiary bank.
Composite Rating	The holding company's overall condition and potential impact on the U.S. financial system.
Depository Institution	This rating is derived from the subsidiary bank's examination and is essentially the same as the bank's primary regulator's rating.

Larger holding companies are generally examined once a year, while smaller ones are generally examined on a bi-annual basis, with thresholds based on asset size generally established at the $100 billion, $10 billion, and $3 billion levels.

IDI Examinations

IDIs are examined first and foremost for their safety and soundness, but also on a variety of other matters. National banks and federal thrifts are examined by the OCC. State banks will be examined by both their primary federal regulatory agency and the appropriate state department of financial institutions. Depending on the state and condition of the IDI, these examinations may run concurrently, or the agencies may alternate years. Specialized agencies also have limited examination authority.

Safety and Soundness Examinations

The purpose of safety and soundness examinations is to evaluate the overall financial condition of a bank or savings and loan association (referred to collectively as "IDIs" in this chapter). IDIs are generally required to undergo a full scope, on-site safety and soundness examination every 12 months, except for certain eligible institutions that are examined every 18 months.[4]

4. *See, e.g.*, 12 U.S.C. § 1820(d). *See, also*, Federal Reserve, SR 18-7: Updates to the Expanded Examination Cycle for Certain State Member Banks and U.S. Branches and Agencies of Foreign Banking Organizations (Jan. 23, 2019).

Uniform Financial Institutions Rating System. Examiners assign to IDIs examination ratings that are based on the Uniform Financial Institutions Rating System (**UFIRS**). Under UFIRS, an IDI is examined based on an evaluation of six financial and operational components: **C**apital Adequacy, **A**sset Quality, **M**anagement, **E**arnings, **L**iquidity, and **S**ensitivity to Market Risk (collectively, "**CAMELS**").

Each component of the CAMELS rating is also based on the "1" to "5" scale, and some components may be given more weight than others depending on the IDI's size, complexity of operations, and risk profile. A rating of "1" indicates superior condition and "5" shows a strong likelihood of failure.

Read about CAMELS and ratings at https://www.occ.treas.gov/publications-and-resources/publications/economics/working-papers-banking-perf-reg/pub-econ-working-paper-camels-ratings.pdf. See also: FDIC Risk Management Manual of Examination Policies, Federal Deposit Insurance Corporation, Basic Examination Concepts and Guidelines, Section 1.1-20.

CAMELS System. The components of the CAMELS system are:

Component	Coverage
Capital Adequacy	An institution's ability to maintain capital commensurate with its risks.
Asset Quality	The quantity of existing and potential credit risk associated with loan and investment portfolios, other real estate owned, other assets, and off-balance sheet transactions. This usually involves a review of a sampling of loans, and the examiners will challenge management on the collectability of the loans.
Management	The capability of the board of directors and management to identify, measure, monitor, and control the risks of an IDI's activities, and to ensure an IDI's safe, sound, and efficient operation in compliance with applicable laws and regulations.
Earnings	The quantity, trend, and factors that may affect the sustainability or quality of earnings, often based on comparability to peers.

Liquidity	The adequacy of an IDI's liquidity position, with consideration given to the current level and prospective sources of liquidity compared to funding needs, and the adequacy of funds management practices relative to the IDI's size, complexity, and risk profile.
Sensitivity to Market Risk	The degree to which changes in interest rates, foreign exchange rates, commodity prices, or equity prices can adversely affect an IDI's earnings or economic capital.

Composite Rating. Under the UFIRS, as noted above, each IDI is assigned a composite of "1" to "5" based on the evaluation and rating of each of the six individual CAMELS components. These ratings are:

Rating	
Composite 1	A rating of "1" indicates that an IDI is sound in every respect and generally has components rated "1" or "2." Any weaknesses are minor and can be handled in a routine manner by the board of directors and management.
Composite 2	An institution with a composite rating of "2" is fundamentally sound. For an IDI to receive this rating, generally no component rating should be more severe than "3." In addition, an IDI with a "2" rating has only moderate weaknesses that are well within the board of directors' and management's capabilities and willingness to correct. These IDIs have no material supervisory concerns and, as a result, the supervisory response is informal and limited.
Composite 3	Banks that are rated "3" exhibit some degree of supervisory concern in one or more of the component areas and exhibit a combination of weaknesses that may range from moderate to severe; however, the magnitude of the deficiencies generally will not cause a component to be rated more severely than a "4." Management may lack the ability or willingness to effectively address weaknesses within appropriate timeframes. Banks in this group generally are less capable of withstanding business fluctuations than those IDIs rated a composite rating of "1" or "2."

Composite 4	These IDIs generally exhibit unsafe and unsound practices or conditions. There are serious financial or managerial deficiencies that result in unsatisfactory performance. The problems range from severe to critically deficient. The weaknesses and problems are not being satisfactorily addressed or resolved by the board of directors and management. Banks in this group generally are not capable of withstanding business fluctuations and there may be significant noncompliance with laws and regulations. Risk management practices are generally unacceptable relative to the IDI's size, complexity, and risk profile. Close supervisory attention is required, which means, in most cases, formal enforcement actions are necessary to address the problems. Banks in this group pose a risk to the Deposit Insurance Fund. Failure is a distinct possibility if problems and weaknesses are not satisfactorily addressed and resolved.
Composite 5	These IDIs exhibit extremely unsafe and unsound practices or conditions; exhibit a critically deficient performance; and often contain inadequate risk management practices relative to the IDI's size, complexity, and risk profile. In addition, the volume and severity of problems are beyond management's ability or willingness to control or correct. Immediate outside financial or other assistance is needed in order for the IDI to be viable. Ongoing supervisory attention is necessary. Banks in this group pose a significant risk to the Deposit Insurance Fund and failure is highly probable.

Reports of Examination. Examination findings are issued in a confidential Report of Examination (**ROE**) to the IDI. The IDI's overall composite rating, and particularly its management component, also reflect its scores on compliance and specialty examinations.

"Well Managed." One of the requirements for FHCs and financial subsidiaries is that the holding company and its subsidiary IDIs be "well managed." This means that each has a composite examination rating of 2 or better and a management rating of 2 or better.

Other Types of Examinations

There are other examinations, sometimes by the same regulator, but the examiners will have expertise in the subject matter of the exam, and sometimes by another regulatory body.

Consumer Compliance and CRA. Consumer compliance and CRA examination cycles are based on an IDI's size and the IDI's previous consumer compliance rating.[5]

These exams cover:

Type of Exam	Coverage
Consumer Compliance	*FDIC, Compliance Examination Manual, Overview of Compliance Examinations, Section II-12; Supervision and Examination Manual, CFPB, Part I.* Banking agencies utilize compliance examinations as the primary means to determine whether an IDI is meeting its responsibility to comply with the requirements of federal consumer protection laws and regulations. The CFPB examines IDIs with over $10 billion in consolidated assets for consumer compliance, while the appropriate primary federal IDI regulatory agencies examine smaller institutions. Ratings for consumer compliance examinations are based on the Uniform Interagency Consumer Compliance Rating System. Under this system, an IDI is assigned a consumer compliance rating predicated on an evaluation of the nature and extent of its present compliance with consumer protection and civil rights statutes and regulations, and the adequacy of its operating systems. The rating system is based on a scale of "1" to "5" in increasing order of supervisory concern. Thus, "1" represents the highest rating and consequently the lowest level of supervisory concern, while "5" represents the lowest, most critically deficient level of performance, and therefore the highest degree of supervisory concern.

5. FDIC, Compliance Examination Manual, Examination and Visitation Frequency, Section II-11.

Community Reinvestment Act	*http://www.ffiec.gov/cra/default.htm* The Community Reinvestment Act (CRA) encourages IDIs to help meet the credit needs of the communities in which they operate, including low- and moderate-income neighborhoods, consistent with safe and sound banking operations. Banking agencies are required to evaluate IDIs' compliance with the CRA periodically. This evaluation is publicly available and is referred to as a "public evaluation." The IDI's rating, which may be "Outstanding," "Satisfactory," "Needs to Improve," or "Substantial Noncompliance," is included in the public evaluation. The public evaluation is taken into account in considering an institution's applications for branching and other expansionary activities.

Specialty Examinations. The regulatory agencies also conduct a number of specialty examinations that focus on one area of law or one aspect of banking.

Type of Exam	Coverage
Bank Secrecy Act of 1970 and Anti-Money Laundering	*https://bsaaml.ffiec.gov/manual* The purpose of the Currency and Foreign Transactions Reporting Act of 1970 (commonly known as the "Bank Secrecy Act" or "**BSA**"), which was substantially amended and enhanced by the Uniting and Strengthening America by Providing Appropriate Tools Required to Intercept and Obstruct Terrorism Act of 2001 (commonly known as the "USA PATRIOT Act"), is to ensure that banks maintain appropriate records and file certain reports involving currency transactions and an IDI's customer relationships, and that these records and reports are sufficient enough to reconstruct the transactions, if necessary. These records and reports have a high degree of usefulness in criminal, tax, money laundering, illegal drug and terrorist financing, and regulatory investigations or proceedings.

	Findings from BSA examinations are generally included within the safety and soundness examination; however, separate BSA examinations can be conducted. Adverse BSA findings can affect both the safety and soundness management rating and the overall composite rating of the institution. They also must be factored into approvals on applications for mergers and acquisitions.
Trust and Fiduciary	*FDIC, RMS Manual of Examination Policies, Basic Examination Concepts and Guidelines, Section 1.1-15 to 1.1-16.* *Federal Financial Institutions Examination Council, Uniform Interagency Trust Rating System, Notice, 63 Fed. Reg. 54,704 (Oct. 13, 1998).* A bank's trust department acts in a fiduciary capacity when the assets that it manages are not the bank's but belong to and are for the benefit of others. This type of relationship necessitates a great deal of confidence on the part of customers, and it demands a high degree of good faith and responsibility on the bank's part. The primary objective of a trust department examination is to determine whether its operations, or the administration of its accounts, give rise to possible or contingent liabilities, or direct liabilities (estimated losses), which could reduce the bank's capital accounts. Examinations of trust activities are conducted and scored on the basis of the Uniform Interagency Trust Rating System (**UITRS**) adopted by the FFIEC in 1998. The UITRS has five components: **M**anagement Ability; **O**perations, Internal Controls, and Auditing; **E**arnings; **C**ompliance; and **A**sset Management (collectively, "MOECA"). Each of these components and the composite rating are based on a scale of "1" to "5," with a "1" being the highest rating and indicating the strongest performance and risk management practices and the least degree of supervisory concern. Banking agencies generally conduct trust examinations on the same cycle as safety and soundness examinations.

Information Technology	*https://www.ffiec.gov/cyberassessmenttool.htm* *https://www.occ.gov/news-issuances/bulletins/2015/bulletin-2015-31.html* *https://www.federalreserve.gov/supervisionreg/srletters/sr1509.htm* Information technology (**IT**) services apply to virtually all recordkeeping and operational areas in banks. These IT services may be managed internally on an IDI's own in-house computer system, or outsourced, wholly or in part, to an independent data center that performs most IT functions. Although some or all IT services may be outsourced, management and the board retain oversight responsibilities. IT has become an ever-increasing area of critical concern for the banking agencies, given recent publicized data breaches, cyber-attacks on banks, and related cybersecurity issues. The potential consequences of receiving faulty data, suffering an interruption of services, or a cyber-attack are serious, and warrant comprehensive IT policies and procedures and thorough IT examinations. A primary objective of an IT examination is to determine the confidentiality, integrity, and availability of records produced by automated systems. Examination priorities include an evaluation of management's ability to identify risks and maintain appropriate compensating controls. IT operations are generally evaluated on the basis of the FFIEC Information Technology Examination Handbook. Recently, the FFIEC also introduced the Cybersecurity Assessment Tool (**CAT**). The CAT is meant to be used by banks to assess their cybersecurity preparedness, but as discussed below, the banking agencies are trending toward using the CAT as an examination tool.

	IT operations are rated in accordance with the Uniform Rating System for Information Technology (**URSIT**), which is based on an evaluation of four critical components: audit; management; development and acquisition; and support and delivery. The composite IT rating is influenced by the performance of the four component functions and reflects the effectiveness of an IDI's IT risk management and information security programs and practices. A scale of "1" through "5" is used, wherein "1" indicates strong performance and "5" denotes critically deficient operating performance. Most IT examinations are embedded in risk management ROEs and only include an URSIT composite rating. Banking agencies may, however, direct examiners to conduct full-scope IT examinations that include composite and component ratings. Banking agencies generally conduct IT examinations on the same cycle as safety and soundness examinations. Nevertheless, the banking agencies are trending toward utilizing the CAT in IT examinations.
Financial Technology ("fintech")	Financial Technology ("**fintech**") is a new area for both IDIs and the bank regulatory agencies, and as such, is a new area for examinations. As more IDIs utilize fintech as a solution or offer banking-as-a-service (BaaS) to fintechs, the federal bank regulatory agencies are conducting fintech-focused examinations. Although there are no uniform requirements for fintech examinations, guidance is drawn from various IT, third-party relationships, and vendor management guidance. Fintech examinations are evolving, but nevertheless, the federal bank regulatory agencies in fintech examinations have focused on BSA/AML issues, compliance management system evaluations, board and senior management education and involvement, sufficiency of IDI infrastructure, fintech-related policies and procedures, and third-party relationships.

Post-Examination Actions

Lots of information is available on post-examination:

OCC Bulletin 2018-18, Comptroller's Handbook Examination Process series: Updated Booklets and Rescissions, (June 28, 2018), available at https://www.occ.treas.gov/news-issuances/bulletins/2018/bulletin-2018-18.html;

Federal Reserve, SR 13-13, Supervisory Considerations for the Communication of Supervisory Findings (June 17, 2013), available at https://www.federalreserve.gov/supervisionreg/srletters/sr1313.htm.

FDIC, RMS Manual of Examination Policies, Section 16.1-1.

In addition to a composite rating, an examination may result in the banking regulator directing the holding company or IDI to address Matters Requiring Immediate Attention (**MRIAs**) or Matters Requiring Attention (**MRAs**). MRIAs are, as the name suggests, matters that an IDI must immediately address, while MRAs are less critical and more time is allowed to rectify the particular issue.

Confidentiality of Supervisory Ratings and Other Nonpublic Supervisory Information

All bank regulatory agencies, including the CFPB and the states, have rules on confidentiality or ROE finding and ratings. For example, read the Federal Reserve regulations on the confidentiality of these materials at 12 C.F.R. Part 261, Subpart C.

ROEs are confidential and are the property of the agency issuing the report. Accordingly, the written approval of the issuing agency is generally required to disclose to third parties such reports or the information derived from them, as well as other information broadly deemed to be nonpublic supervisory information. There are exceptions related to disclosure to the IDI's holding company, insiders, and certain advisors. The inappropriate disclosure or use of nonpublic supervisory information may subject individuals to certain criminal penalties.[6]

It may not appear to rank up there in severity or complexity with safety and soundness and prudential regulation at first blush, but the bank regulatory agencies take a fierce stance on confidentiality of ROEs, examination ratings, and other nonpublic supervisory materials—so serious in fact that the Federal Reserve Board on August 3, 2016, ordered Goldman Sachs Group to pay a $36.3 million civil money penalty for its unauthorized use and disclosure of

6. 18 U.S.C. § 641.

confidential supervisory information, and to implement an enhanced program to ensure the proper use of confidential supervisory information.[7] As scary, the Federal Reserve Board announced that it was instituting enforcement proceedings against a former managing director at Goldman Sachs, seeking to impose a fine and permanently bar him from the banking industry stemming from his and his subordinates' unauthorized use and disclosure of confidential supervisory information.[8] States have the same sensitivity. Goldman had earlier (October 28, 2015) reached a settlement agreement with the New York State Department of Financial Services in connection with the unauthorized possession of its confidential supervisory information.[9]

Appeals of Material Supervisory Determinations

Each of the federal banking agencies must establish an independent intra-agency appellate process to review material supervisory determinations made at the insured depository institutions that it supervises.[10]

> *The law requires each federal agency to appoint an ombudsman to act as a liaison between the agency and any affected person with respect to any problem that party may have in dealing with the agency resulting from the regulatory activities of the agency, and to assure that safeguards exist to encourage complainants to come forward and preserve confidentiality.*
>
> *An example: FDIC FIL-42-2017, Revised Guidelines for Appeals of Materially Supervised Determinations, (Sept. 6, 2017), https://www.fdic.gov/news/news/financial/2017/fil17042.html.*

Material supervisory determinations include all of the ratings addressed above, as well as:

- ALLL adequacy determinations;
- significant loan classifications;
- determinations relating to violations of a statute or regulation that may affect the capital, earnings, or operating flexibility of an institution, or otherwise affect the nature and level of supervisory oversight accorded an institution;
- Truth in Lending (Regulation Z) restitution;
- decisions to initiate informal enforcement actions (such as memoranda of understanding);

7. *See,* In the Matter of the Goldman Sachs Group, Inc. New York, New York and Goldman, Sachs & Co, New York, New York 2016 WL 4432523 (Aug. 2, 2016); *see also,* http://www.federalreserve.gov/newsevents/press/enforcement/20160803a.htm.
8. *Id.*
9. *See,* http://www.dfs.ny.gov/about/press/pr1510281.htm.
10. 12 U.S.C. § 4806(a).

- determinations regarding the institution's level of compliance with a formal enforcement action; however, if the FDIC determines that the lack of compliance with an existing formal enforcement action requires additional enforcement action, the proposed new enforcement action is not appealable;
- matters requiring board attention; and
- any other supervisory determination (unless otherwise not eligible for appeal) that may affect the capital, earnings, operating flexibility, or capital category for prompt corrective action purposes of an institution, or otherwise affect the nature and level of supervisory oversight accorded an institution.

Material supervisory determinations do *not* include:

- decisions to appoint a conservator or receiver for an insured depository institution;
- decisions to take prompt corrective action pursuant to Section 38 of the Federal Deposit Insurance Act;
- determinations for which other appeals procedures exist (such as determinations of deposit insurance, assessment risk classifications, and payment calculations);
- decisions to initiate informal enforcement actions, as discussed below; and
- formal enforcement actions and decisions, *including determinations and the underlying facts and circumstances that form the basis of a recommended or pending formal enforcement action*, and agency determinations regarding compliance with an existing formal enforcement action.

A formal enforcement action or decision commences, and, therefore, becomes unappealable, when the applicable federal agency initiates a formal investigation or provides written notice to the institution indicating its intention to pursue a formal enforcement action.

Regulatory Enforcement Actions

When a bank regulatory agency determines—typically, but not necessarily, in connection with an examination—that an institution's overall financial condition has deteriorated, and/or that one or more of its CAMELS component ratings have decreased, such that a composite and/or component rating of "3" is warranted, the agency is likely to impose, or otherwise require the institution to enter into, an enforcement action.[11] This action will allow the agency to direct and monitor the activities to be taken or avoided by the institution to correct the identified issues. Enforcement actions may also arise from practices or activities deemed to be unsafe and unsound, or that represent a breach of a fiduciary duty.

Regardless of the nature and terms of an enforcement action, it should be taken seriously by the institution's board of directors, management, and advisors, as it reflects an unsatisfactory condition or an unsafe and unsound practice that must be remedied or ceased before the applicable agency will be willing to terminate the enforcement action and its related requirements and restrictions, which can be quite onerous and resource consuming. With knowledge of the legal foundations of, and regulatory practices related to, enforcement actions, a legal practitioner can, however, help to reduce the adverse impact of an enforcement action on an institution, and in some cases, reduce the severity of certain terms or the overall nature of the enforcement action.

Overview

Regulatory enforcement actions are considered to be either "informal" or "formal." Informal enforcement actions are normally associated with less serious regulatory issues and reflect an IDI's willingness to self-correct those issues, rather than the largely involuntary and directive-based nature of formal enforcement actions. Accordingly, informal enforcement actions are generally corrective in nature, whereas formal enforcement actions may also be punitive in nature or include such elements.

Typically, the terms of informal enforcement actions that involve safety and soundness and/or compliance issues closely resemble the terms of formal enforcement actions. The primary difference between informal and formal enforcement actions is that informal enforcement actions are considered to be confidential supervisory information that is not, and generally may not, be publicly disclosed,[12] whereas a formal enforcement action is published by each applicable regulator on its website and otherwise. Moreover, formal enforcement actions have statutory roots, mechanisms, and implications, whereas informal enforcement actions generally do not. Accordingly, material noncompliance, even if involuntary, with the terms of an informal enforcement action will often

11. *See* FDIC Formal and Information Enforcement Actions Manual; OCC Bulletin 2018-41, *Enforcement Action Policies and Procedures Manuals* (Nov. 13, 2018), available at https://www.occ.treas.gov/news-issuances/bulletins/2018/bulletin-2018-41.html.
12. In certain instances, however, federal securities laws may permit and/or require the disclosure of certain information pertaining to enforcement actions.

result in the imposition of a formal enforcement action to provide for greater supervisory oversight.

Because national banks and federal thrifts are not directly regulated by the states, the OCC will typically be the sole regulatory agency involved in enforcement actions related to such institutions. Similarly, the applicable Federal Reserve Bank will generally be the sole regulator with respect to enforcement actions involving a BHC. Also, the applicable federal regulator will often be the sole agency involved with a consumer compliance enforcement action. Notwithstanding the typically joint nature of enforcement actions, sometimes a state bank's federal and state regulators do not always reach the same preliminary or final conclusion regarding the condition of an IDI and the warranted enforcement action, if any.

Importantly, when a target IDI is presented with a proposed informal enforcement action, or if the target is willing to stipulate or consent to the issuance of a formal enforcement action (as further described below), the applicable regulatory agencies are generally willing to engage in discussions and negotiations with the target and its legal advisors regarding the nature and terms of the enforcement action. It should be noted, however, that more discussion, negotiation, and resultant change is permitted in connection with proposed informal enforcement actions. The formal enforcement actions issued by each federal agency generally reflect the same form and content, although the agencies may be willing to consider changes to items, such as the time permitted for completion of, or compliance with, certain requirements, or the dollar threshold for loan review or workout plan requirements, for example.

Obviously, the more severe the issues relating to an enforcement action target, the less amenable to negotiation the agencies will be, notwithstanding the target's contrition and/or cooperation. Accordingly, an IDI regulatory lawyer must understand and be fully aware of the challenges and issues facing the target institution, so that any discussions and negotiations with the applicable regulatory agencies can yield the most favorable result for the target institution.

As described below, there is a hierarchy of severity for both informal and formal enforcement actions.

Informal Enforcement Actions

Informal enforcement actions, in order of ascending severity, generally consist of corrective board resolutions or memoranda of understanding. They are nonpublic.

Corrective Action	
Corrective Board Resolutions	These are the least severe of all enforcement actions. They are often developed with the significant involvement, and adopted at the strong direction, of the institution's regulator(s). Notwithstanding this regulatory involvement, the primary advantage of corrective board resolutions over other forms of enforcement actions is that they have the external appearance of originating solely from the institution, rather than being imposed by the institution's regulator(s).
Memorandum of Understanding	A Memorandum of Understanding (MOU) is the most severe form of informal enforcement action and is likely to be imposed on any institution that has received a composite CAMELS rating of "3" and/or if the institution has deficiencies in other areas that warrant direction and close supervision by regulators. An MOU is essentially a contractual agreement between an institution and its regulator(s) that sets forth specific corrective actions to be taken or restrictions to be observed by the institution. Like contracts, MOUs are generally executed by representatives of the institution and each applicable regulatory agency.

Formal Enforcement Actions

As discussed above, formal enforcement actions constitute more severe, and public, remedial and restrictive actions against an institution or an institution-affiliated party (**IAP**)[13] by banking regulators and are generally imposed when the related deficiencies or violations are more serious or have not been satisfactorily resolved under a previous informal enforcement action.

Really important note: *lawyers are considered IAPs.*

Moreover, and also as noted above, formal enforcement actions are either: (i) corrective, and thus direct an IDI to take, or refrain from, certain actions; or (ii) punitive, which impose monetary penalties and/or have a prohibitive impact with respect to individuals.

13. 12 U.S.C. § 1818(b)(7). The definition of an IAP is set forth in 12 U.S.C. § 1813(u).

There is a federal statutory framework for formal enforcement actions, and each federal banking agency has policies and practices that supplement this framework and that address informal enforcement actions. Additionally, in most instances, there are state law equivalents (which are beyond the scope of this book) for each type of enforcement action; accordingly, enforcement actions are typically issued jointly, where applicable. For example, enforcement actions involving state nonmember banks will generally be imposed or entered into by the FDIC and the applicable state banking agency, whereas the applicable state banking agency and the Federal Reserve Bank will impose or enter into enforcement actions with respect to state member banks.

The rules, mechanisms, and implications relating to formal enforcement actions are primarily prescribed in Section 8 of the FDIA, which is codified at 12 U.S.C. § 1818.

In sum, Section 1818 provides:

Enforcement Action	
Written Agreements	Written agreements are bilateral contractual agreements between a federal regulator and an institution or an IAP, the structure and terms of which are typically very similar to MOUs. In response to violations of, or substantial noncompliance with, written agreements, federal regulators may issue or impose more stringent enforcement actions, as described below. Written agreements are generally treated and enforceable as cease-and-desist orders under the FDIA.

<table>
<tr>
<td>Cease and Desist/ Consent Orders</td>
<td>Under federal law, the federal banking regulators may issue cease-and-desist orders (a C&D) that prohibit, restrict, or require certain activities or functions of an institution or an IAP. In addition, through or in connection with a C&D, the federal banking regulators have broad authority to require the subject of a C&D to:
<ul>
<li>make restitution or provide reimbursement, indemnification, or guarantee against loss if the institution or the subject was unjustly enriched in connection with the violation or practice at issue, or if the violation or practice involved a reckless disregard for the law or any applicable regulations or prior order;</li>
<li>restrict the institution's growth (as applicable);</li>
<li>dispose of any loan or asset involved;</li>
<li>rescind agreements or contracts;</li>
<li>employ qualified officers or employees (who may be subject to approval by the applicable federal regulator); and</li>
<li>take such other action as the federal regulator determines to be appropriate.</li>
</ul>
Notably, during the last banking crisis, if target state nonmember banks stipulated (i.e., consented) to the issuance of a C&D, the FDIC began referring to, and labeling, such enforcement actions as "consent orders."[14] This nuanced change by the FDIC served to synchronize the apparent practice of each of the federal banking agencies to generally label a C&D as such only when a target does not stipulate to its issuance or if the basis for the order is particularly egregious.</td>
</tr>
</table>

14. Consent orders are therefore, for all practical purposes, C&Ds, and enforced accordingly.

Temporary Cease and Desist Orders	The federal banking regulators may also issue temporary C&Ds, which become immediately effective and remain until the federal regulator either rescinds the order or issues a standard C&D or other formal enforcement action to replace the temporary C&D. The actions or omissions that warrant temporary C&Ds are those that are likely to: • cause an institution's insolvency or a significant dissipation of an institution's assets or earnings; • weaken the institution's condition; or • prejudice the interests of an institution's depositors. The subject of a temporary C&D may seek review of it by the appropriate U.S. District Court, within 10 days of the imposition of such order. Similarly, federal banking regulators may apply to the applicable U.S. District Court to enforce a temporary C&D.
Removal, Suspension, and Prohibition Orders	The federal regulators are also authorized by law to issue removal, suspension, and prohibition orders against IAPs regarding their current or future bank-related responsibilities. The criteria for issuing a removal order consist of whether the subject institution-affiliated party has: • violated any law, regulation, final C&D order, written regulatory application condition, or formal written agreement; • engaged or participated in any unsafe or unsound practice; or • committed or engaged in an activity or an omission that constitutes a breach of the IAP's fiduciary duty.

<table>
<tr><td></td><td>The applicable federal regulator next must determine whether the activity or omission resulted in:<ul><li>actual or potential financial loss or damage;</li><li>prejudice to the interests of the institution's depositors; or</li><li>the IAP receiving financial gain or other benefit as a result of such activity or omission.</li></ul>Lastly, the federal regulator must demonstrate that the activity or omission at issue involved personal dishonesty or demonstrated a willful or continuing disregard for the safety and soundness of the institution.

Although removal orders involve the process and determinations described above, suspension orders against IAPs are effective immediately, much like temporary C&Ds.

Federal banking regulators also have the authority to suspend or prohibit an IAP from further participation in any manner in the conduct of the affairs of any depository institution.</td></tr>
<tr><td>Civil Money Penalties</td><td>Depending on the nature and severity of committed violations, federal law authorizes the federal banking regulators to issue civil money penalties (CMPs) against institutions and IAPs. CMPs are structured into three tiers, based on the severity of the violation(s).

First-tier CMPs of up to $5,000 per day; Second-tier CMPs of up to $25,000; and Third-tier CMPs of up to the lesser of $1 million or 1% of the institution's total assets per day, subject to a limit of $1 million for individuals, may be issued against an institution or IAP based on specific criteria.</td></tr>
</table>

Prior to imposing a CMP, the applicable federal regulator will provide the institution or IAP with what is commonly known as a "15-day letter," which gives the target an opportunity to submit relevant information to the agency prior to the ultimate CMP assessment decision. When determining whether to assess a CMP and the amount thereof, the federal regulators will consider:

- the size of financial resources and good faith of the insured depository institution or other person charged;
- the gravity of the violation;
- the history of previous violations; and
- such other matters as justice may require.

The banking agencies utilize various matrices for assessing CMPs against financial institutions and IAPs.[15] Ultimately, the amount of a CMP should both serve a remedial purpose and provide a deterrent to future misconduct.

Procedural Matters Relating to Formal Enforcement Actions

Stipulation Agreement

A proposed formal enforcement action will typically be accompanied by a proposed stipulation agreement. A stipulation agreement allows the banking regulator to impose a formal enforcement action without the issuance of a notice of charges and the administrative law process described below. By stipulating (*i.e.*, consenting) to the issuance of the enforcement action, the target is not required to admit wrongdoing and avoids the public disclosure of the specific examination or other findings that the IDI's regulator(s) deem severe enough to warrant the issuance of an enforcement action. In addition, stipulation will generally result in substantial cost and time savings that would be incurred if the matter were to proceed to an administrative hearing.

If the target of a formal enforcement action agrees to execute a stipulation agreement, the target must agree to waive certain rights to which the target would otherwise be entitled, such as:

- the issuance of a formal notice of charges by the regulator;
- an administrative law hearing and the final agency decision on the matter;
- judicial review of the administrative law and agency decision;
- contesting the validity of the enforcement action;

15. Federal Financial Institutions Examination Council, Interagency Policy Regarding the Assessment of Civil Money Penalties by the Federal Financial Institutions Regulatory Agencies, 63 Fed. Reg. 30,227 (June 3, 1998); *see also,* OCC Bulletin 2018-41, *infra.*

- claims for fees, costs, or expenses against the regulator; and
- assertion of a "double jeopardy" claim in the event of a criminal prosecution.

As noted above, because stipulation prevents the facts, circumstances, and issues that are the basis for the proposed enforcement action from being made public, and reduces the expenditure of time and funds, the vast majority of formal enforcement actions are issued via stipulation of the target. Moreover, and also as discussed above, a target's willingness to stipulate to a formal enforcement action will generally allow the target and its legal advisors to discuss and negotiate the provisions of the enforcement action with the issuing regulator(s).

Notice of Charges

Because of the serious nature and implications of formal enforcement actions, the target of any such action is statutorily provided the opportunity to request both administrative and judicial review of the issuance of the formal enforcement action. As part of this legal process, prior to the issuance of a non-stipulated formal enforcement action, the applicable federal banking regulator is required to provide the target of the action with a notice of charges.[16] The notice of charges will contain a recitation of the facts surrounding the alleged violations or practices, and must set forth a date and venue for an administrative hearing regarding the appropriateness of the issuance of the formal enforcement action.[17] The administrative hearing will generally be scheduled for 30 to 60 days from the service of the notice of charges, unless the parties agree otherwise.

Because issuing a notice of charges results in the public disclosure of the facts and circumstances relating to the alleged violations and/or unsafe and unsound practices, the vast majority of institutions and institution-affiliated parties that are the targets of formal enforcement actions attempt to confidentially negotiate the terms of these actions and then stipulate or consent to the issuance of the action (and thus forego the notice of charges and administrative hearing), as described above. Accordingly, challenging a formal enforcement action through the statutorily provided administrative and judicial process should generally be reserved for instances in which the target has strong facts to demonstrate that the regulatory agency's findings and proposed enforcement action are arbitrary and capricious, an abuse of discretion, or unconstitutional, for example.[18]

16. 12 U.S.C. § 1818(b)(1), (e)(4).

17. *Id.*

18. 5 U.S.C. § 706(2).

Administrative Review

If an IDI believes that the issuance of a formal enforcement action against it constitutes, *inter alia*, an arbitrary and capricious act by a banking regulator and is willing and able to expend the time and funds, the IDI may request an administrative hearing to contest the issuance of the formal enforcement action. Each of the federal banking regulators has promulgated regulations that direct the administrative hearing process related to a contested formal enforcement action.[19] These regulations address issues such as informal settlement procedures, discovery, motions, and conflicts of interest. The Office of Financial Institution Adjudication (**OFIA**) oversees the administration of enforcement hearings by the federal banking regulators. An administrative law judge from the OFIA conducts the administrative law hearings related to contested formal enforcement actions.

Judicial Review

Judicial review of the issuance of formal enforcement actions, which can occur only after the completion of the administrative law procedure described above, is extremely rare. Moreover, a banking lawyer and his or her client should recognize that federal courts give tremendous deference to administrative interpretation and decisions.

If the result of an administrative hearing is that the appropriateness of a formal enforcement action is confirmed, upon issuance of the final enforcement action, it will generally remain effective and enforceable until it is "stayed, modified, terminated or set aside by action of the agency or a reviewing court."[20]

The federal Administrative Procedures Act sets forth the criteria for reversing the final decision of federal banking regulators. These criteria, which represent a high and difficult threshold for the target of a formal enforcement action to overcome, allow the reviewing court to reverse the regulator's decision only if, after reviewing the entire record, the court determines that the agency's decision was:

- arbitrary, capricious, an abuse of discretion, or otherwise not in accordance with law;
- contrary to constitutional right, power, privilege, or immunity;
- in excess of statutory jurisdiction, authority, or limitations, or short of statutory right;
- without observance of legal procedure;
- unsupported by substantial evidence; or

19. *See*, 12 C.F.R. Part 308 (FDIC); 12 C.F.R. Part 263 (Federal Reserve); 12 C.F.R. Part 19 (OCC); 12 C.F.R. Part 1081 (CFPB).

20. 12 U.S.C. § 1818(b)(2).

- unwarranted by the facts to the extent that the facts are subject to trial *de novo* by the reviewing court.[21]

Publication

Once a federal banking regulator has finalized and issued a formal enforcement action, federal law requires the publication of the action.[22] The federal banking regulators may delay the publication of an action for a reasonable amount of time if the publication of the action in accordance with the regulator's normal timing and procedures would present a serious threat to the target or related institution's safety and soundness.[23] Publications of certain actions may be avoided altogether if the publication would be contrary to the public interest.[24] Moreover, competitive disadvantage or the potential for an adverse liquidity event (*i.e.*, a run on the bank) will generally *not* constitute a sufficient reason for a federal banking regulator to delay or avoid the publication of a formal enforcement action.[25] Accordingly, to the extent possible and permitted, the legal practitioner should diligently attempt to negotiate the language in, and terms of, formal enforcement actions.

Indemnification

Federal law and regulations generally prohibit a financial institution from indemnifying an IAP for the liability or legal expense in connection with an enforcement action or civil action brought by a federal banking regulator that results in the issuance of a C&D, removal or prohibition order, or civil money penalty against the IAP.[26] A financial institution may, however, purchase an insurance policy or fidelity bond that will pay for the legal or professional expenses incurred by an IAP in connection with the defense of an enforcement action, or with respect to restitution of the financial institution, but this policy or bond may not provide reimbursement for any final judgment or civil money penalty.[27] Of note, there is no ban on an IAP purchasing his or her own insurance policy for a potential CMP or reimbursement for a final judgment.

21. 5 U.S.C. § 706(2).
22. 12 U.S.C. § 1818(u)(1).
23. 12 U.S.C. § 1818(u)(4).
24. 12 U.S.C. § 1818(u)(1)(A).
25. In fact, we are not aware that a publication delay based on these factors has ever been granted.
26. *See, e.g.*, 12 C.F.R. §§ 359.1(l)(1), 359.3.
27. *See, e.g.*, 12 C.F.R. § 359.1(l)(2)(i).

In addition, a financial institution *may* indemnify an IAP for legal or professional expenses relating to violations for which the IAP was ultimately determined not to be responsible.[28] Notwithstanding the foregoing, an institution may also indemnify a target IAP for expenses (but not for the payment of a civil money penalty or restitution) related to a formal enforcement action prior to the "commencement" of such action, which is deemed to be the issuance of a notice of charges.[29]

28. *See, e.g.*, 12 C.F.R. § 359.1(l)(2)(ii), FDIC FIL-47-2013, *Director and Officer Liability Insurance Policies, Exclusions, and Indemnification for Civil Money Penalties* (Oct. 10, 2013), available at https://www.fdic.gov/news/news/financial/2013/fil13047.html.

29. Federal Deposit Insurance Corporation, Regulation of Golden Parachutes and Other Benefits Which May Be Subject to Misuse, 60 Fed. Reg. 16,069, 16,077 (Mar. 29, 1995), 61 Fed. Reg. 5,926, 5,930 (Feb. 15, 1996).

Banking Law: Acronyms, Lingo, and Jargon

Banking Term	Reference	Definition	Chapter[1]
§ 24 (Seventh)	12 U.S.C. § 24 (Seventh)	The general powers authority for national banks that requires their activities to be the "business of banking" or "incidental thereto." Many state banks have the same powers by virtue of state parity or wild card statutes.	3
ACH	Automated Clearing House	A processing network whereby interbank transactions are cleared through batch electronic file entries. The ACH Network allows billions of direct deposit and direct payment transactions to be sent in account-to-account transfers.	
Advanced Approaches		Refers to the large or "core" international banks (generally defined for U.S. purposes as having total assets of $250 billion or more, or consolidated foreign exposures of $10 billion or more) that are subject to Basel II and are required to hold additional capital buffers.	6
AIB	American Institute of Banking	Provides specialized education and training for bankers.	
ALLL	Allowance for Loan and Lease Losses	The reserve financial institutions must maintain against loan and lease losses. It is a contra account on the asset side of the bank balance sheet to reduce gross loans to net loans and absorb loan and lease losses.	5, 6
AML	Anti-Money Laundering	Usually referred to with the Bank Secrecy act as "AML-BSA," part of the regulatory regime aimed at money laundering, terrorist financing, tax evasion, and other criminal activities.	3, 8

1. The indication of a chapter(s) relates to the primary focus in *Banking Law Essentials* on the topic. It is not exclusive. The term may not appear in the Table of Contents for the referenced chapter.

Banking Term	Reference	Definition	Chapter[1]
AOCI	Accumulated Other Comprehensive Income	A bank earnings entry that reflects unrealized gains and losses on bank available-for-sale securities. Under Basel III, AOCI flows through capital unless the bank opted out in the first quarter of 2015.	
ATR	Ability to Repay	Required by sections 1411 and 1412 of Dodd-Frank and the CFPB's amendments to Reg Z, which generally compel creditors to make a reasonable, good faith determination of a consumer's ability to repay any consumer credit transaction secured by a dwelling (excluding an open-end credit plan, timeshare plan, reverse mortgage, or temporary loan) and establishes certain protections from liability under this requirement for "qualified mortgages." See QM.	
BaaS	Banking as a Service	A fintech term comprising relationships with banks where the fintech provides banking services to its customers.	
Bank-eligible	12 U.S.C. § 24 (Seventh) 12 C.F.R. Part 1	Refers to the types of securities in which banks may invest under 12 C.F.R. Part 1 (generally high-grade debt instruments).	5
BASEL	The Basel Committee on Banking Supervision	Provides a forum for cooperation on banking supervisory matters. Its objective is to enhance understanding of key supervisory issues and improve the quality of banking supervision worldwide. It seeks to do so by exchanging information on national supervisory issues, approaches, and techniques, with a view to promoting common understanding. At times, the Committee uses this common understanding to develop guidelines and supervisory standards in areas where they are considered desirable. The Committee is best known for its international standards on capital adequacy; the Core Principles for Effective Banking Supervision; and the Concordat on cross-border banking supervision.	6

Banking Term	Reference	Definition	Chapter[1]
BASEL I	The original Basel Committee Framework for Capital Adequacy	The original risk-based capital guidelines, based upon the 1988 capital accord adopted by the international Basel Committee on Banking Supervision. It imposed minimum capital standards on banks and thrifts, and, for the first time, it required a risk-weighting of assets in connection with the calculation of required capital ratios. It also required off-balance sheet exposures to be weighted and brought back on the balance sheet.	
BASEL II	The Basel II Framework for Capital Adequacy	In 2008, the U.S. banking agencies collaboratively began to phase-in capital standards based on a second capital accord, referred to as "Basel II," for Advanced Approaches institutions. Basel II emphasized internal assessment of credit, market and operational risk, as well as supervisory assessment and market discipline in determining minimum capital requirements.	
BASEL III	The Basel III Framework for Capital Adequacy	The capital reform implemented internationally in response to the Global Financial Crisis. The rules require banks and holding companies to hold more and better-quality capital. The U.S. Basel III rules became effective on January 1, 2015. See Reg Q, 12 C.F.R. 217.	6
BHC	Bank Holding Company	Any entity "controlling" a financial institution whose deposits are insured by the Federal Deposit Insurance Corporation. See also FHC.	4
BHCA	Bank Holding Company Act of 1956 12 U.S.C § 1841 et seq	Contains relevant definitions and governs the activities of companies that control banks, including Bank Holding Companies and Financial Holding Companies.	4
BHCA § 3	12 U.S.C. § 1842	The section of the BHCA that applies to companies becoming BHCs and acquiring banks.	4

Banking Term	Reference	Definition	Chapter[1]
BHCA § 4(c) (8)	12 U.S.C. § 1843(c)(8)	The section of the BHCA that restricted BHC's to activities "closely related to banking or a proper incident thereto." The list of activities permitted under 4(c)(8) was frozen by Gramm-Leach-Bliley. It is in Reg Y at 12 C.F.R. 225.28.	4
BIF	Bank Insurance Fund	Created by FIRREA; the part of the FDIC insurance fund that insured the deposits of banks as opposed to thrifts. Now combined with SAIF as one DIF fund.	
BIS	Bank for International Settlements	Owned by 63 central banks from around the world that meet on a regular basis in Basel, Switzerland. Founded in 1930, the mission of BIS "is to serve central banks in their pursuit of monetary and financial stability, to foster international cooperation in those areas and to act as a bank for central banks." The Basel Committee on Bank Supervision is a part of BIS.	6
BMA	Bank Merger Act	A part of the FDIA and NBA that provides the rules for banks to merge and consolidate.	
Board	Board of Governors of the Federal Reserve System	Overall governing board of the various Federal Reserve banks located around the country and responsible for U.S. monetary policy. Also the regulatory authority for BHCs and THCs and primary federal regulator of state banks that are members of the Federal Reserve System. See Fed and FRS.	2, 4
BOLI	Bank-Owned Life Insurance	Refers to limited types of life insurance that banks and thrifts may legally own. Such products may not be held for investment purposes but may be held to hedge liabilities, for instance employee benefit obligations of a bank/thrift. The bank regulatory agencies have released interagency guidance on BOLI.	

Banking Term	Reference	Definition	Chapter[1]
BOPEC	**B**anks, **O**ther Subsidiaries, **P**arent, **E**arnings, **C**apital	The former examination rating system used by the Fed for bank holding companies.	
BSA	Bank Secrecy Act of 1970	Requires financial institutions to keep records of cash purchases of negotiable instruments, file reports of cash transactions exceeding $10,000 (daily aggregate amount), and to report suspicious activity that might signify money laundering, tax evasion, or other criminal activities.	8
Bureau	Bureau of Consumer Financial Protection	See CFPB.	2
C&D	Cease and Desist Order	Issued by regulators to a bank, thrift, holding company or its Institution Affiliated Parties (Officers, Directors, etc.) to require affirmative action or stopping actions that violate law or are unsafe and unsound.	8
C&I	Commercial and Industrial	Bank commercial loans.	
Call Report	Periodic Reports of Condition	Quarterly financial report filed by financial institutions.	5
CAMELS	**C**apital Adequacy, **A**sset quality, **M**anagement, **E**arnings, **L**iquidity and Market **S**ensitivity	The examination rating system used by bank regulatory agencies with numerical ratings of 1-5. 1 is best, 5 is worst.	8
CARD Act (or Credit CARD Act)	Credit Card Responsibility and Disclosure Act of 2009	Addresses abuses in credit card practices including imposing limits on changes in terms and raising rates; limits fees and expiration dates on gift cards.	

Banking Term	Reference	Definition	Chapter[1]
CARES Act	Coronavirus Aid, Relief, and Economic Security Act of 2020	The $2 trillion coronavirus economic stimulus bill, signed into law by President Trump on March 27, 2020. The Act included elements aimed at helping keep people engaged in the economy with direct cash for many, plus expanded unemployment benefits and loans to small and large businesses.	
CBLR	Community Bank Leverage Ratio	Basel III "off-ramp" for institutions with total consolidated assets of less than $10 billion provided by Section 201 of the Regulatory Relief Act. The banking agencies set the CBLR at 9% of tangible equity to total assets for a qualifying bank to be well capitalized. A community banking organization is eligible to elect the framework if it has less than $10 billion in total consolidated assets, limited amounts of certain assets and off-balance sheet exposures, and a CBLR greater than 9%. The electing institution would not be required to calculate the existing risk-based and leverage capital requirements of the Basel III Rule and would not need to risk weight its assets for purposes of capital calculations.	6
CCAR	Comprehensive Capital Analysis and Review	A supervisory assessment by the Fed of the capital planning processes and capital adequacy of the larger, complex BHCs (over $250 billion). One component is testing against a severely adverse macroeconomic scenario specified by the Fed. It is intended to demonstrate that the banks have robust, forward-looking capital planning processes that account for their unique risks and sufficient capital to continue operations throughout times of economic and financial stress.	
CCyB	Countercyclical Buffer	A capital buffer, intended to operate as an additional amount of the Capital Conservation Buffer for Advanced Approaches institutions.	6

Banking Term	Reference	Definition	Chapter[1]
CDD	Customer Due Diligence	Required as a part of AML-BSA compliance, a bank's responsibility to verify the identity of a bank customer. It is the process where relevant information about the customer is collected and evaluated for any potential risk for the organization or money laundering/terrorist financing activities.	
CDFI	Community Development Financial Institutions	Program to use federal resources to invest in and build the capacity of CDFIs to serve low-income people and communities lacking adequate access to affordable financial products and services.	
CDO	Collateralized Debt Obligation	A type of derivative, used to repackage individual loans into a product that can be sold to investors on the secondary market.	
CDS	Credit Default Swaps	A swap agreement between two counter parties. "Covered CDS" are purchased by a buyer with an interest in the underlying reference obligation as a hedge against the buyer's risk of loss on such reference obligation. A buyer may purchase a CDS on a reference entity in which the buyer does not hold any interest, in order to speculate (rather than hedge against the risk of loss) on the future creditworthiness of the reference entity (e.g., buying a CDS on a security issued by an entity in financial distress).	
CEBA	Competitive Equality Banking Act of 1987	Established new standards for expedited funds availability; recapitalized the Federal Savings & Loan Insurance Company (FSLIC); expanded FDIC authority for open bank assistance transactions, including bridge banks.	

Banking Term	Reference	Definition	Chapter[1]
CECL	Current Expected Credit Loss	CECL is a controversial GAAP accounting standard adopted by FASB in the wake of the Global Financial Crisis that changes how depository financial institutions of any size account for expected credit losses. CECL requires financial institutions to record "life of loan" loss estimates at origination or purchase. This replaces the "incurred loss" accounting model and changes the way in which financial institutions manage the ALLL by requiring forecasting on loan performance. It also applies to credit losses on held-to-maturity securities. CECL took effect in Q1 2020 for large IDIs with holding companies that are registered with the SEC. Effectiveness was otherwise delayed for smaller reporting BHCs and banks and credit unions until 2023. The CRES Act included a further optional delay for two years.	5
CET 1	Common Equity Tier 1	Basel III not only increased most of the required minimum capital ratios, but it also introduced the concept of "Common Equity Tier 1 Capital," which consists primarily of common stock, related surplus (net of Treasury stock), retained earnings, and Common Equity Tier 1 minority interests, subject to certain regulatory adjustments. As of January 1, 2015, the Basel III Rule requires CET 1 to risk-weighted assets of 4.5%.	6
CFPB	Bureau of Consumer Financial Protection	The Bureau that operates as an independent part of the Federal Reserve and regulates consumer financial products and certain providers of such products under Title X of Dodd-Frank. Its regulations are codified at 12 C.F.R. 1000 et seq.	2

Banking Term	Reference	Definition	Chapter[1]
C.F.R.	Code of Federal Regulations	Federal banking regulations are codified in 12 C.F.R. under the part assigned to the federal banking regulator promulgating the regulation. Certain interpretations of statutes are also included in 12 C. F. R.	2
Check 21	Check Clearing for the 21st Century Act 12 C.F.R. 229	A federal law that allows banks to handle paper checks electronically through check images and has given rise to remote and mobile deposit of checks and the use of substitute checks and image replacement documents in connection with check clearing and settlement.	
CIP	Customer Identification Procedures	Know your customer requirements imposed by the USA Patriot Act. See KYC.	8
CLA	Consumer Leasing Act	Provides for uniform disclosure of terms and costs of consumer leases; similar to Truth in Lending; requires lease agreements to include certain terms, including a statement of the number of lease payments and their dollar amounts, penalties for not paying on time and whether a lump sum payment is due at the end of the agreement.	
CLAR	Comprehensive Liquidity Analysis and Review	A supervisory assessment by the Federal Reserve of the liquidity planning processes of the larger, complex BHCs.	
CMP	Civil Money Penalty	Fines imposed by regulators against financial institutions and IAPs under the FDIA.	8
Comptroller	Comptroller of the Currency	The Comptroller is the chairman of the Office of the Comptroller of the Currency, which charters and regulates all national banks and federal thrifts.	2, 3
Collins Amendment	DFA § 171(b)	A provision of DFA that requires bank and thrift holding companies (except those with under $3 billion in assets) to hold capital on a consolidated basis as stringent as that required for insured depository institutions.	

Banking Term	Reference	Definition	Chapter[1]
Correspondent Bank		Depository institutions hold deposits of each other and provide services to others and to their customers. These arrangements are generally contractual in nature and involve banks as "correspondents" of each other. Upstream correspondent banks provide services to smaller institutions, known as downstream correspondents.	
Council	Financial Stability Oversight Council	See FSOC.	
CP	Commercial Paper	Short-term corporate debt of less than 9 months' duration.	
CRA	1. Community Reinvestment Act 2. Consumer Reporting Agency	1. Requires a financial institution to provide lending and banking services to the entire community it serves, in particular to low- and medium-income neighborhoods. It is the subject of a separate compliance exam by the applicable regulator with exam ratings: outstanding, satisfactory (high and low), needs to improve, and substantial noncompliance. Unlike other exam ratings, CRA ratings are published. The Act permits protests to be filed in connection with certain merger and acquisition applications. 2. Companies that collect information and provide reports on consumers that are used to decide whether to provide consumers credit, insurance, or employment, and for other purposes. Equifax, Experian, and TransUnion and the large national CRA's.	4, 8

Banking Term	Reference	Definition	Chapter[1]
Crapo	The Economic Growth, Regulatory Relief and Consumer Protection Act of 2018	Also known as the "Regulatory Relief Act," Crapo was enacted in May of 2018 to modify or remove certain financial reform rules and regulations. The law roles back a number of Dodd-Frank provisions, especially dealing with community and regional banks: the SIFI test was increased to \$250 billion (from \$50 billion); less than \$10 billion are generally exempt from Volcker Rule and risk committee requirement; between \$50 billion and \$100 billion are exempt from enhanced prudential standards (resolution planning, stress tests, single-party credit limits) immediately and no longer subject to stress testing; less than \$10 billion may adopt CBLR only (off-ramp for Basel III) of 9% (as set by agencies); small BHC rules apply to \$3 billion and less; mortgage relief; and reciprocal deposit relief from brokered deposit restrictions.	
CRE	Commercial Real Estate	Generally, refers to commercial lending secured by real property. The bank regulatory agencies have released guidelines for banks to develop risk management practices and levels of capital that are commensurate with the level and nature of their concentrations.	
CSBS	Conference of State Bank Supervisors	A clearinghouse for ideas to solve common problems of state bank regulators and to advocate for the continuation of the Dual Banking System.	
CSI	Confidential Supervisory Material	The regulatory agencies view any information included in an examination report (including CAMELS ratings), and any information derived therefrom to be confidential. They also consider informal enforcement proceedings and information gathered from investigations as CSI. Sharing of this information without permission of the regulatory agency is a violation of Federal law.	8

Banking Term	Reference	Definition	Chapter[1]
CTR	Currency Transaction Report	A report that U.S. financial institutions are required to file for each deposit, withdrawal, exchange of currency, or other payment or transfer, by, through, or to the financial institution that involves a transaction in currency of more than $10,000.	8
CUNA	Credit Union National Association	Non-governmental, not-for-profit, trade group representing and lobbying for credit unions.	
CUSO	Credit Union Service Organization	Subsidiaries of credit unions that may engage in a broader range of activities than the credit union itself.	3
DCC	Debt Cancellation Contracts	A type of credit insurance recognized as not being insurance by the banking agencies. DCC's are a contract between the financial institution and the debtor pursuant to which debt is paid off a death or disability, and sometimes on termination of employment. OCC regulations on the product are in 12 CR Part 37.	
DDA	Demand Deposit Account	A transaction deposit account—better known as a checking account.	5
de novo	Latin: new	Used as a reference to newly formed banks and newly formed branches.	
DFA	The Dodd-Frank Wall Street Reform and Consumer Protection Act of 2010	See Dodd-Frank.	
DFAST	Dodd-Frank Annual Stress Testing	A test that banks with total consolidated assets of more than $100 billion must run annually against a severely adverse macroeconomic scenario to determine the ability of the financial institution to deal with an economic crisis. Required by Section 165(i)(2) Dodd-Frank.	

Banking Term	Reference	Definition	Chapter[1]
DIDMCA	Depository Institutions Deregulation and Monetary Control Act of 1980	Federal law that established "NOW Accounts." Began the phase-out of interest rate ceilings on deposits. Established the Depository Institutions Deregulation Committee. Granted new powers to thrift institutions. Raised the deposit insurance ceiling to $100,000.	
DIF	Deposit Insurance Fund	The DIF is administered by the FDIC and provides deposit insurance for all insured banks and thrifts in the U.S. Various categories of deposits are insured up to $250,000.	
Discount Window		Credit facilities in which financial institutions go to borrow funds from the Federal Reserve. These loans, which are priced at the discount rate, are often structured as secured loans to alleviate pressure in reserve markets. It helps to reduce liquidity problems for banks and assists in assuring the basic stability of financial markets.	
Dodd-Frank	The Dodd-Frank Wall Street Reform and Consumer Protection Act of 2010	The major financial reform package enacted in 2010, Dodd-Frank boasts 16 titles and creates 13 new Federal offices, with its principal mission to prevent systemic risk from threatening the financial system.	2
DPC	Debt Previously Contracted	Property that banks are permitted to own for a limited number of years after they take it as collateral for a loan that defaults.	5
DRP	Disaster Recovery Plan	IDIs and their vendors are required to maintain and test DRPs for business continuity.	
DRR	Designated Reserve Ratio	The FDIC manages the DIF with a DRR goal as a percentage of insured deposits. The current goal is to obtain a DRR of 2%.	

Banking Term	Reference	Definition	Chapter[1]
Dual Banking System		A system of bank regulation unique to the United States whereby banks may be chartered either by each of the 50 states and territories or by the federal government, and each of those jurisdictions has certain regulatory controls over the banks and charters. Also true of savings and loan associations and credit unions.	1, 3
ECOA	Equal Credit Opportunity Act	Consumer protection statute with implementing regulations that prohibits discrimination in lending practices.	
EDD	Enhanced Due Diligence	As a part of AML-BSA compliance, bank due diligence policies, procedures, and processes should be enhanced for customers that pose higher money laundering or terrorist financing risks present increased exposure to banks.	
EDGE	Edge Act Corporation	Created by the Edge Act, § 25 of the Federal Reserve Act, it is a subsidiary of a bank, federally chartered by the Fed, which is established in the United States to offer services to only non-US residents and institutions. The services offered include deposit and loan services. Implementing regulation is Reg K (12 C.F.R. Part 211) under the Federal Reserve Act. It is a subsidiary of a bank.	
EESA	Emergency Economic Stability Act of 2008	Created TARP and guarantee programs to stabilize the economy during the Global Financial Crisis.	
EFTA	Electronic Fund Transfer Act Reg E (12 C.F.R. Part 1005)	Establishes the rights and liabilities of consumers as well as the responsibilities of all participants in EFT activities; provides for the establishment of minimum standards for the transmission of funds electronically and provides for the establishment of regulations to deal with the manner and effect of such transfers.	

Banking Term	Reference	Definition	Chapter[1]
EPS	Enhanced Prudential Standards	Section 165 of the Dodd-Frank Act required the Board to establish enhanced prudential standards for bank holding companies and foreign banking organizations with total consolidated assets of $50 billion (changed to some $100 billion and all $250 billion by Crapo) or more and nonbank financial companies that were designated by FSOC for supervision by the Board. The standards include enhanced risk-based and leverage capital, liquidity, risk management and risk committee requirements; a requirement to submit a resolution plan; single-counterparty credit limits; stress test requirements; and others as the Board determines.	4
eSLR	Enhanced Supplementary Leverage Ratio	A rule to strengthen the leverage ratio standards for the largest, most interconnected U.S. banking organizations. It applies to U.S. top-tier bank holding companies with more than $700 billion in consolidated total assets or more than $10 trillion in assets under custody (covered BHCs) and their insured depository institution (IDI) subsidiaries (the 8 large U.S. banking organizations meet the size thresholds and their IDI subsidiaries). Covered BHCs must maintain a leverage buffer greater than 2 percentage points above the minimum supplementary leverage ratio requirement of 3 percent, for a total of more than 5 percent, to avoid restrictions on capital distributions and discretionary bonus payments. IDI subsidiaries of covered BHCs must maintain at least a 6 percent supplementary leverage ratio to be considered "well capitalized" under the agencies' prompt corrective action framework.	4

Banking Term	Reference	Definition	Chapter[1]
FACT Act	Fair and Accurate Credit Transactions Act of 2003	Extensive amendments to the then existing Fair Credit Reporting Act to improve the accuracy and transparency of the national credit reporting system, prevent identity theft, and assist victims; restricts sharing of consumer information among affiliates without an opt out; contains provisions enhancing consumer rights in situations involving alleged identity theft, credit scoring, and claims of inaccurate information; allows consumers to request and obtain a free credit report once every 12 months from each of the 3 nationwide consumer credit reporting companies (Equifax, Experian, and TransUnion).	
FASB	Federal Accounting Standards Board	The organization primarily involved in developing Generally Accepted Accounting Principles.	
FBO	Foreign Banking Office(s)	Refers to a foreign banking office of a domestic bank.	
FCRA	Fair Credit Reporting Act	Consumer protection statute and regulations relating to the reporting of credit history.	
FDCPA	Fair Debt Collection Practices Act	Provides rules for debt collection practices under regulations of the CFPB.	
FDIA	Federal Deposit Insurance Act of 1950	Revised and consolidated earlier FDIC legislation into one act. Embodies the basic authority for the current operation of the FDIC.	2, 3
FDIC	Federal Deposit Insurance Corporation	Provides federal insurance for deposits of virtually all commercial banks and thrifts (i.e., savings banks and savings and loans) and serves as receiver in bank and thrift failures. The FDIC is also the principal federal regulator of state-chartered banks that are not members of the Federal Reserve System and state-chartered thrifts.	2, 3

Banking Term	Reference	Definition	Chapter[1]
FDICIA	Federal Deposit Insurance Corporation Improvement Act of 1991	Increased the powers and authority of the FDIC; recapitalized the Bank Insurance Fund; created new supervisory and regulatory examination standards; established new capital requirements for banks; ordered the creation of a risk-based deposit insurance assessment scheme; mandated a least-cost resolution method and prompt resolution approach to problem and failing banks; and created new Truth in Savings provisions. Also limited the authority of state banks and their subsidiaries to act as principal in activities prohibited to national banks without approval of the FDIC, and prohibited insurance underwriting through state banks, except to the extent permitted to national banks.	2, 3
Fed or Federal Reserve	Federal Reserve System	Refers to the central bank of the U. S. comprised of the Board and 12 Federal Reserve Banks. Also the regulatory authority for BHCs and THCs and the primary federal regulator of state banks that are members of the Federal Reserve System. See FRS.	2, 3, 4, 8
Federal Funds Rate		A fluctuating interest rate per annum equal to the weighted average of the rates on overnight Federal Funds transactions with members of the Federal Reserve System that are arranged by Federal funds brokers, all as published for a particular day by the Federal Reserve Bank of New York.	
FEMA	Federal Emergency Management Agency	Oversees the National Flood Insurance Program, which requires participating communities to adopt and enforce ordinances that meet or exceed FEMA requirements to reduce the risk of flooding. See NFIP.	

Banking Term	Reference	Definition	Chapter[1]
FFIEC	Federal Financial Institutions Examination Council	Interagency body composed of the FED, FDIC, and OCC empowered to prescribe uniform principles, standards, and report forms for the federal examination of financial institutions regulated by each of them and to make recommendations to promote uniformity in the supervision of financial institutions; was given additional statutory responsibilities by section 340 of the Housing and Community Development Act of 1980 to facilitate public access to data that depository institutions must disclose under HMDA, as well as the aggregation of annual HMDA data, by census tract, for each metropolitan statistical area.	8
FHC	Financial Holding Company	A bank holding company that has requested and qualified to become a financial holding company and that has elected to engage in "financial activities" as defined in the Gramm-Leach-Bliley Act. In effect, it is a holding company that may have subsidiaries engaged in commercial banking, investment banking, and insurance. It and its subsidiary banks/thrifts must be well capitalized, well managed, and in compliance with CRA and must maintain compliance with those tests or be subject to loss of powers.	4
FHFA	Federal Housing Finance Agency	The independent agency created in 2008 to regulate and supervise the GSEs. See FHFB.	
FHFB	Federal Housing Finance Board	Created by FIRREA. Is under HUD and supervises the 12 FHLB's.	
FHLB	Federal Home Loan Banks	12 Regional Banks regulated by FHLBB until FIRREA. Now regulated by Federal Housing Finance Board. Primarily serve as source of residential mortgage credit.	

Banking Term	Reference	Definition	Chapter[1]
FHLBB	Federal Home Loan Bank Board	Established in 1932 as the regulator of federal and state savings and loan associations or "thrifts." FIRREA replaced it with the OTS.	
FHLMC	Federal Home Loan Mortgage Corporation	Commonly known as Freddie Mac, it is a federal government-sponsored enterprise (GSE) of the United States Government authorized to make loans and loan guarantees. Freddie Mac buys mortgages on the secondary market, pools them, and sells them as mortgage-backed securities to investors on the open market.	
FICO	The Financing Corporation	A mixed-ownership governmental corporation chartered by the former Federal Home Loan Bank Board pursuant to the Competitive Equality Banking Act of 1987 to function as a financing vehicle for the recapitalization of the former FSLIC. FICO issued 30-year noncallable bonds of approximately $8.1 billion that matured in September 2019. FICO's authority to issue bonds ended on December 12, 1991. Since 1996, federal legislation has required that all FDIC-insured depository institutions pay assessments to cover interest payments on FICO's outstanding obligations. The final payment was in March of 2019.	
FinCEN	Financial Crimes Enforcement Network	The U.S. Department of the Treasury established the Financial Crimes Enforcement Network in 1990 to provide a government-wide multisource financial intelligence and analysis network. The organization's operation was broadened in 1994 to include regulatory responsibilities for administering the Bank Secrecy Act.	2, 8

Banking Term	Reference	Definition	Chapter[1]
FIO	Federal Insurance Office	Created by Dodd-Frank as a part of Treasury. Its mandate is not to be a regulator or supervisor—that role stays with the states—but to monitor all aspects of insurance, assist Treasury and coordinate efforts in certain respects, recommend insurers who may be nonbank companies subject to supervision by the Federal Reserve, make preemption determinations, and consult with state insurance regulators.	
FINRA	Financial Industry Regulatory Authority	The largest self-regulatory organization (SRO) for broker-dealers. It was created in July 2007 through the consolidation of the National Association of Securities Dealers (NASD) and the member regulation, enforcement, and arbitration functions of the New York Stock Exchange. Broker-dealers and their registered representatives and associated persons must hold licenses issued by FINRA, for instance Series 7 and 24. FINRA produces and enforces the FINRA Rulebook.	
Fin Sub	Financial Subsidiary	A type of subsidiary of a bank created by the Gramm-Leach-Bliley Act that has greater securities powers than the parent bank. The bank must be well capitalized and well managed to own a fin sub and must meet other prudential requirements.	3
FIRIRCA	Financial Institutions Regulatory and Interest Rate Control Act of 1978	Created the FFIEC. Established limits and reporting requirements for bank insider transactions. Created major statutory provisions regarding electronic fund transfers.	

Banking Term	Reference	Definition	Chapter[1]
FIRREA	Financial Institutions Reform, Recovery, and Enforcement Act of 1989	Abolished FSLIC and gave FDIC the responsibility of insuring the deposits of thrift institutions in its place; created the Savings Association Insurance Fund (SAIF) as part of the FDIC insurance fund to cover thrifts, while the fund covering banks was called the Bank Insurance Fund (BIF) and was kept separately; abolished the FHLBB and created two new agencies, the Federal Housing Finance Board (FHFB) and the Office of Thrift Supervision (OTS), to replace it; created RTC as a temporary agency to manage the assets of failed thrifts.	2
FNMA	Federal National Mortgage Association	Commonly known as Fannie Mae, FNMA is a GSE that purchases qualifying residential home mortgages on the secondary market, pools them, and sells them as mortgage-backed securities to investors on the open market.	
FOMC	Federal Open Market Committee	Part of the Federal Reserve Board that sets economic policy.	
FRS	Federal Reserve System	The central banking system of the United States. It is a quasi-public (government entity with private components) banking system composed of (i) the presidentially appointed Board of Governors of the Federal Reserve System in Washington, D.C.; (ii) the Federal Open Market Committee; (iii) 12 regional Federal Reserve Banks located in major cities throughout the nation acting as fiscal agents for the U.S. Treasury; (iv) numerous private U.S. member banks, which subscribe to required amounts of non-transferable stock in their regional Federal Reserve Banks; and (v) various advisory councils.	2, 3, 4

Banking Term	Reference	Definition	Chapter[1]
FSA	Federal Savings Association	A federal depository institution charter originally established to focus on consumer real estate lending under the Home Owners' Loan Act. Chartered by and regulated by the OTS before Dodd-Frank and the OCC after July 21, 2011. Also, an abbreviation that a federal saving association can use in its name.	1, 2, 3
FSB	Federal Savings Bank	A federal depository institution charter originally established to focus on consumer real estate lending under the Home Owners' Loan Act. Chartered by and regulated by the OTS before Dodd-Frank and the OCC after July 21, 2011. Also, an abbreviation that a federal saving association can use in its name.	1, 2, 3
FSLIC	Federal Savings & Loan Insurance Corporation	A subsidiary of the FHLBB that provided deposit insurance to S&L's. Abolished by FIRREA, it was replaced by the FDIC as insurer of all U.S. deposits.	2
FSOC	Financial Stability Oversight Council	Council created by Title I of Dodd-Frank and chaired by the Secretary of the Treasury. It is composed of representatives from the principal federal financial regulatory agencies and a representative of the insurance industry, with its principal mission to prevent systemic risk from threatening the financial system. In so doing, the Council will fill gaps in supervision, monitor financial market developments, identify emerging risks in firms and market activities, and facilitate coordination of interagency policy and resolution of disputes.	2
GAAP	Generally Accepted Accounting Principles	Accounting standards adopted by FASB.	

Banking Term	Reference	Definition	Chapter[1]
Garn-St Germain	Garn-St Germain Act	Deregulated the limitations of S&Ls to take demand deposits and establish money market accounts; S&Ls were authorized to make commercial, corporate, business, or agricultural loans up to 10% of assets; expanded the powers of thrift institutions into a broader scope of activities and limited the insurance powers of bank holding companies; expanded FDIC powers to assist troubled banks.	2
Glass-Steagall	Glass-Steagall Act	Established the FDIC as a temporary agency. Separated commercial banking from investment banking, establishing them as separate lines of commerce. Gramm-Leach-Bliley revised and eliminated most of the Glass-Steagall act relating to affiliations between investment banking organizations and commercial banks. The provisions dealing with limitations on bank activities were not modified by GLBA.	2
GLBA	Gramm-Leach-Bliley Act of 1999	Repealed most of the Glass Steagall Act of 1933. Allows national banks to underwrite municipal bonds. Allows FHCs to engage in underwriting and selling insurance and securities, conducting both commercial and merchant banking, investing in and developing real estate and other "complementary activities." Preserves authority of states to regulate insurance but prohibits state actions that have the effect of preventing bank-affiliated firms from selling insurance on an equal basis with other insurance agents. Makes significant changes in the operation of the Federal Home Loan Bank System, easing membership requirements and loosening restrictions on the use of FHLB funds. Restricts the disclosure of nonpublic customer information by financial institutions.	2

Banking Term	Reference	Definition	Chapter[1]
GSE	Government-Sponsored Enterprise	Entities that are government related: Freddy Mac, Fanny Mae, and the Federal Home Loan Banks	
G-SIB	Global Systemically Important Bank	A financial institution whose distress or disorderly failure, because of its size, complexity, and systemic interconnectedness, would cause significant disruption to the wider financial system and economic activity. They must hold additional loss absorption capacity tailored to the impact of their default, to be met with common equity. The list is updated from time to time and includes JPMorgan Chase, Citigroup, and Bank of America.	4
Hedge		An investment strategy to reduce the risk of adverse price movements in an asset. A hedge consists of taking an offsetting position in a related security, such as a futures contract.	
Hedge Fund		An investment vehicle that pools capital from a number of investors and invests in securities and other instruments. They are administered by a professional management firm, and are often structured as a limited partnership, limited liability company, or similar vehicle. They are typically structured to avoid registration under the federal securities laws.	
HMDA	Home Mortgage Disclosure Act of 1975	Establishes minimum and uniform disclosures of the terms and related charges for home mortgages.	

Banking Term	Reference	Definition	Chapter[1]
HOEPA	Home Ownership and Equity Protection Act of 1994	Amends TILA to require additional disclosures and additional protections for closed end not-purchase money mortgages on principal residences; targets high-interest and high-fee loans mainly in the home equity area. Assignees of such loans are also liable for penalties. Fed issues regs defining rates that trigger the applicability and setting forth of required disclosure forms and information.	
HOLA	Home Owners' Loan Act	Established the savings association charter and provides the rules for their supervision and regulation. The OCC now is the regulator with supervisory responsibility.	2, 3
HQLA	High-Quality Liquid Assets	A liquidity objective arising from the Global Financial Crisis to provide an incentive for banks and holding companies to increase their holdings in unencumbered high-quality liquid assets like Treasury securities and other sovereign debt as a component of assets.	
IAP	Institution Affiliated Party	Officers, Directors, Principal Shareholders, and Independent Contractors (which can include attorneys and accountants under some situations). The banking regulators may take enforcement actions against IAPs in certain circumstances, including imposing CMPs.	8
IBF	International Banking Facility	A banking entity that any U.S. bank, or a U.S. branch/subsidiary of a foreign bank, or an Edge Act Corporation establishes in the United States to offer services to only non-U.S. residents and institutions. The services offered include deposit and loan services.	
IDI	Insured Depository Institution	Refers to banks and thrifts, any financial institution with FDIC-insured deposits. Frequently used in rulemaking by the banking agencies.	1

Banking Term	Reference	Definition	Chapter[1]
IHC	Intermediate Holding Company	As part of the Dodd-Frank Act's enhanced prudential standards, foreign banking organizations with $50 billion or more in U.S. non-branch/agency assets were required to place virtually all U.S. subsidiaries underneath a top-tier U.S. intermediate holding company. IHC's are subject to U.S. Basel III, capital planning, Dodd-Frank stress-testing, liquidity, risk management requirements, and other U.S. EPS on a consolidated basis.	
ILC	Industrial Loan Company	State-chartered institutions that originated in the early 1900s as finance companies for lower-income borrowers. ILCs were chartered in seven states as of mid-2004: California, Colorado, Hawaii, Indiana, Minnesota, Nevada, and Utah. These early ILCs offered relatively high-interest unsecured loans to factory workers who could not otherwise obtain credit. They were not originally FDIC insured and, for historical reasons, may be owned by commercial companies.	1, 3, 4
KYC	Know Your Customer	The due diligence that financial institutions and other regulated companies must perform to identify their clients and ascertain relevant information pertinent to doing financial business with them. In the USA, KYC is typically a policy implemented to conform to a customer identification program mandated under the Bank Secrecy Act and USA PATRIOT Act and to prevent identity theft fraud, money laundering, and terrorist financing. It is a process that banks must continually undertake from the start of a customer relationship to the end.	

Banking Term	Reference	Definition	Chapter[1]
LCR	1. Liquidity Coverage Ratio 2. Least Cost Resolution	1. Liquidity is a measure of the ability and ease with which bank assets may be converted to cash. Liquid assets are those that can be converted to cash quickly if needed to meet financial obligations. The LCR is designed to ensure that the banking entity has an adequate stock of unencumbered high-quality liquid assets that can be converted easily and immediately in private markets into cash to meet liquidity needs for a 30-calendar day liquidity stress scenario. The U.S. bank regulatory agencies implemented the LCR in September 2014 for the large banking organizations. 2. Refers to the requirement that the FDIC determine the least costly manner in which to resolve a failed IDI.	
Leverage Ratio		A ratio of Tier 1 capital to book assets used to identify capital adequacy.	6
LFI	Large Financial Institution	A rating system imposed by the Federal Reserve in 2019 that replaces RFI/C(D) for holding companies $100 billion in assets or over. The LFI rating system is designed to: (i) align with current supervisory programs and practices for LFIs; (ii) enhance the clarity and consistency of supervisory assessments and communications of supervisory findings and implications; and (iii) provide greater transparency to firms regarding the supervisory consequences of a given rating.	8

Banking Term	Reference	Definition	Chapter[1]
LH&A	Life, Health, and Accident	Types of insurance some financial institutions and holding companies may sell (depending on the powers of the charter) that cover risks associated with death, accidents, and health. Certain kinds of life insurance with investment characteristics are considered to be NDIPs. Bank sales are subject to Consumer Protections in the Sale of Insurance, adopted by all the agencies. See 12 C.F.R. Part 14 for national banks and federal thrifts.	
Line of Business		Refers to an activity of a company that is reasonably separable. The SEC requires that there be separate breakdowns of key economic data for each line of business of a registered company that accounts for more than 20% of the company's revenues.	
Living Will		Required by Dodd-Frank for the largest institutions. All BHCs with over $250 billion in assets (and on a case-by-case basis, some over $100 billion) are required to submit and obtain approval of a plan to unwind the organization in the event of insolvency.	
LMI	Low and moderate income	Bank lending and investing in LMI neighborhoods is the objective of CRA and fair lending laws.	
Loans to One Borrower	12 USC § 84 for national banks.	The lending limit that a bank may extend credit to one borrower.	7
LTOB	See Loans to One Borrower		7

Banking Term	Reference	Definition	Chapter[1]
MBS	Mortgage-Backed Security	An asset-backed security that is secured by a mortgage, or more commonly a collection of hundreds of mortgages. The mortgages are sold to a group that "securitizes," or packages, the loans together into a security that can be sold to investors. In the U.S., they may be issued by government-sponsored enterprises like Fannie Mae or Freddie Mac, or they can be "private-label," issued by structures set up by investment banks.	
Member bank	Member of FRS	State banks that choose to become members of the FRS and have the Fed as their primary federal regulator. They purchase stock in the FRB in their area to become members.	2, 3
MMDA	Money Market Deposit Account	A type of savings account under Reg D.	5
MOU	Memorandum of Understanding	Agreement between regulator and institution regarding required change in practices and operations.	8
MRA	Matter Requiring Attention	An examiner instruction to management of an examined entity to correct a violation of law or other commission or omission.	1, 8
MRC	Minimum Required Capital	Refers to the capital needed to be held by IDIs and holding companies to be adequately capitalized.	6
MRIA	Matter Requiring Immediate Attention	An examiner instruction to management to correct a problem immediately.	1, 8

Banking Term	Reference	Definition	Chapter[1]
MSB	Mutual Savings Bank	These institutions originated in the states and were organized on a philanthropic basis to provide wage earners with a safe place to deposit funds and earn interest. More than 95% of MSBs were concentrated in nine states—Connecticut, Maine, Massachusetts, New Hampshire, New Jersey, New York, Pennsylvania, Rhode Island, and Washington. Many have the power to issue and underwrite Savings Bank Life Insurance, a power not permitted generally to other IDIs.	2
N.A.	National Association	An abbreviation that a national bank can use in its name instead of national bank.	1
NACHA	National Automated Clearinghouse Association	The administrator of the ACH Network. It manages and enforces the ACH Operating Rules and is a payments industry trade association. The NACHA Rules provide the legal foundation for the ACH Network.	
NAFCU	National Association of Federally-Insured Credit Unions	A U.S. trade association of federally insured credit unions.	
NASCUS	National Association of State Credit Union Supervisors	A professional regulators association composed of state credit union regulators that is the primary resource and lobbyist for the 47 state governmental agencies that charter, regulate, and examine the nation's state-chartered credit unions. (Delaware, South Dakota, and Wyoming have no laws permitting state-chartered credit unions.) Also acts as the liaison to federal agencies, including the NCUA.	
NASD	National Association of Securities Dealers	Formerly the SRO for most broker-dealers. Now FINRA.	

Banking Term	Reference	Definition	Chapter[1]
NBA	National Bank Act of 1864	Established a national banking system and the chartering of national banks; established the Office of the Comptroller of the Currency (OCC) as the administrator of national banks.	1, 2, 3
NCUA	National Credit Union Administration; National Credit Union Act	The primary supervisor of federal credit unions. It insures deposits of both state and federal credit unions and the administrator of the National Credit Union Share Insurance Fund (NCUSIF), the insurer of most state-chartered credit unions. The Act establishes and provides authority for NCUA and provides the legal framework for the charter of federal credit unions and the regulation of federal and state credit unions.	2, 3
NCUSIF	National Credit Union Share Insurance Fund	Equivalent of FDIC deposit insurance for customers of credit unions.	3
NDIP	Nondeposit Investment Product	Includes securities, mutual funds, annuities, and life insurance with investment features. Typically referred to in the context of bank direct or indirect sale of the products to retail customers, which is the subject of the Interagency Statement on Retail Sales of Nondeposit Investment Products.	
NFIP	National Flood Insurance Program	Provides a means for property owners to financially protect themselves against floods. The Federal Emergency Management Agency (FEMA) oversees the program, which requires participating communities to adopt and enforce ordinances that meet or exceed FEMA requirements to reduce the risk of flooding. Homeowners must secure the flood insurance policy before closing on a property and renew it every year to cover the principal balance on the loan. When financial institutions make mortgage loans on properties in flood zones, they have an obligation to place flood insurance and force-place such insurance if the mortgagor fails to do so.	

Banking Term	Reference	Definition	Chapter[1]
Nonmember bank		State banks that do not choose to be members of the FRS and have the FDIC as their primary federal regulator.	3
NOW	Negotiable Order of Withdrawal	A type of transaction account like a checking account.	5
NPR	Notice of Proposed Rulemaking	Required by administrative law, it is a notice published in the Federal Register when one of the agencies of the U.S government, including the banking agencies, wishes to add, remove, or change a rule or regulation as part of the rulemaking process. NPR's give the public the opportunity to submit comments that must be considered in connection with final rulemaking.	2
NSF	Non-sufficient Funds (bad check charges)	Refers to a fee charged when there are insufficient funds to settle a check or card obligation.	
OCC	Office of the Comptroller of the Currency	A bureau of the Treasury that charters and supervises national banks and federal thrifts. It has rulemaking authority under the NBA and HOLA.	2, 3
ODP	Overdraft Protection	A service many banks offer so that depositors can overdraw their bank accounts and have the overdraft covered, subject to fees. If structured properly, the service has historically been exempt from federal law regarding consumer open-end credit, but overdrafts of ATM and debit card transactions are subject to an opt-in under Reg E, 12 C.F.R. 1005.	
OFAC	Office of Foreign Assets Control	An agency of the United States Department of the Treasury. OFAC administers and enforces economic and trade sanctions based on U.S. foreign policy and national security goals against targeted foreign states, organizations, and individuals.	
Op Sub	Operating Subsidiary	A subsidiary controlled by a bank or thrift that may only engage in the activities of the parent bank.	3

Banking Term	Reference	Definition	Chapter[1]
OREO	Other Real Estate Owned	Classification for assets of a financial institution acquired in foreclosure of collateral securing a loan.	5
OTS	Office of Thrift Supervision	A part of Treasury that regulated federal thrifts and thrift holding companies and was the federal regulator for state thrifts before the DFA transfer date, when it merged with the OCC.	2
Overdraft		When there are insufficient funds in an account and the bank makes the payment. Overdraft practices and charges are restricted by Reg E.	
Overline	Overline Loan	A loan that exceeds the bank's lending limit.	7
Oversight Council	Financial Stability Oversight Council	See FSOC.	
Part 1	12 C.F.R. Part 1	Generally refers to the regulations of the OCC at 12 C.F.R. Part 1 that restrict the investments national banks, federal thrifts, and state member banks may make. Many state non-member banks are subject to the same rules if state law so provides.	3
P&C	Property and Casualty Insurance	Type of insurance some financial institutions and holding companies may sell that covers risks of destruction or loss of personal and commercial properties. Bank sales are subject to Consumer Protections in the Sale of Insurance, adopted by all the agencies. See 12 C.F.R. Part 14 for national banks and federal thrifts.	

Banking Term	Reference	Definition	Chapter[1]
PCA	Prompt Corrective Action	Federal law provides the federal banking regulators with broad power to take prompt corrective action to resolve the problems of undercapitalized institutions. The extent of the regulators' powers depends on whether the institution in question is "adequately capitalized," "undercapitalized," "significantly undercapitalized," or "critically undercapitalized" in each case as defined by regulation. Depending upon the capital category to which an institution is assigned, the regulators' corrective powers include: (i) requiring the institution to submit a capital restoration plan; (ii) limiting the institution's asset growth and restricting its activities; (iii) requiring the institution to issue additional capital stock (including additional voting stock) or to sell itself; (iv) restricting transactions between the institution and its affiliates; (v) restricting the interest rate that the institution may pay on deposits; (vi) ordering a new election of directors of the institution; (vii) requiring that senior executive officers or directors be dismissed; (viii) prohibiting the institution from accepting deposits from correspondent banks; (ix) requiring the institution to divest certain subsidiaries; (x) prohibiting the payment of principal or interest on subordinated debt; and (xi) ultimately, appointing a receiver for the institution.	6

Banking Term	Reference	Definition	Chapter[1]
PPP	Paycheck Protection Act	A key stimulus program in response to the coronavirus pandemic, PPP was added by Section 1102 of the CARES Act to the Small Business Act. It was designed as an SBA loan to provide direct incentives for small businesses to keep their workers on the payroll. SBA will forgive loans if all employees were kept on the payroll for 8 weeks and the money was used for payroll, rent, mortgage interest, or utilities. The Federal Reserve also created a facility to purchase the loans to allow banks to remove them from their balance sheets.	
QFC	Qualified Financial Contract	Refers to swaps, derivatives, and repurchase agreements that the FDIC must determine to affirm or unwind within 1 day of receivership of a failed IDI.	
QM	Qualified Mortgage	The CFPB's QM requirement implements sections 1411 and 1412 of Dodd-Frank, which generally require creditors to make a reasonable, good faith determination of a consumer's ability to repay (ATR) any consumer credit transaction secured by a dwelling (excluding an open-end credit plan, timeshare plan, reverse mortgage, or temporary loan), and establishes certain protections from liability under this requirement for QMs.	
QTL	Qualified Thrift Lender	A test that savings associations must meet to be regulated as thrifts instead of banks or BHCs. The test requires a majority of assets to be dedicated to mortgage and consumer lending. DFA imposes more severe sanctions on savings associations that do not meet the test, including prohibiting dividend payments to shareholders.	3

Banking Term	Reference	Definition	Chapter[1]
Reg or Reg.	Regulation	Abbreviation used to reference a particular regulation. Bank regulatory agencies promulgate regulations under most statutes for which they have rulemaking authority. Under the Administrative Procedures Act, such proposed regulations are subject to notice and comment. They are published in the Federal Register. Federal banking regulations are codified in 12 C.F.R. in the part dedicated to the regulator promulgating the regulation.	2
Reg B	Equal Credit 12 C.F.R. Part 1002	Former Fed regulation transferred to CFPB that implements the Equal Credit Opportunity Act. The purpose of Reg B is to promote the availability of credit to all creditworthy applicants without regard to race, color, religion, national origin, sex, marital status, or age (provided the applicant has the capacity to contract under state law). The regulation also prohibits the denial of credit merely because an applicant's income is derived from public assistance sources, such as Social Security disability payments. Reg B focuses on the fair treatment of customers in the granting of credit. At its heart, the regulation says the decision to grant credit is to be based on the borrower's ability to meet the lender's credit standards. Matters such as the race, age, or marital status of the borrower or the borrower's reliance on public assistance to repay the loan have no place in the decision to lend.	
Reg C	Home Loan Disclosure 12 C.F.R. Part 1003	Requires banks and thrifts to collect and report information as to loan applications received and mortgage loans made or purchased by them. Information as to income level, race, gender, and other similar information is collected and compared to determine if discriminatory practices exist.	

Banking Term	Reference	Definition	Chapter[1]
Reg D	1. Fed regulation on deposit accounts 12 C.F.R. 204 2. Regulation promulgated by the SEC that constitutes a significant private offering exemption under the Securities Act of 1933	1. Under Fed Reg D, the various kinds of deposit accounts are defined and reserve requirements are established. Also, limitations apply to transaction in savings accounts. 2. Under SEC Reg D substantial amounts of capital may be raised by private sales of equity securities to accredited investors so long as offers to other persons are limited.	5
Reg E	Electronic Funds Transfers 12 C.F.R. Part 1005	Former Fed regulation transferred to CFPB that implements the Electronic Funds Transfer Act. Provides for disclosures and limitations on activities in connection with devices that access accounts. Also implements the CARD Act on gift card limitations and overdraft requirements.	
Reg K	International Banking 12 C.F.R. Part 211	Fed regulation that provides for the regulation of banking activities of U.S. Banks offshore; activities of foreign banks within the U.S.; and sets capital requirements for international structures.	
Reg O	Insider Transactions 12 U.S.C. § 375	Fed regulation implementing legal limitations on loans to officers, directors, and principal shareholder of banks and certain affiliates.	7

Banking Term	Reference	Definition	Chapter[1]
Reg P	Privacy 12 C.F.R. Part 1016	Implements the GLBA Title V privacy provisions by requiring all financial institutions to institute privacy policies with respect to consumer non-public personal information (NPPI) and disclose the same annually and upon account opening. Reg P is for bank holding companies and state member banks. The federal banking agencies have virtually identical regulations.	
Reg Q	Federal Reserve capital rules under Basel III and DFA 12 C.F.R. 217	Provides for the capital regime for U.S. banks, thrifts, and their parent companies effective January 1, 2015. See Basel III.	6
Reg R	Joint Fed/SEC Regulation dealing with Securities Activities of Banks required by GLBA 12 C.F.R. 218 (Fed) 17 C.F.R. 247 (SEC)	Defines the scope of securities activities that banks, thrifts, and credit unions may conduct without registering with the Securities Exchange Commission as a securities broker and implements the most important exceptions from the definition of the term "broker for banks" under section 3(a)(4) of the Securities Exchange Act of 1934. Specifically, the regulation implements the statutory exceptions that allow a bank, subject to certain conditions, to continue to conduct securities transactions for its customers as part of its trust and fiduciary, custodial, and deposit "sweep" functions and to refer customers to a securities broker-dealer pursuant to a networking arrangement with the broker.	
Reg W	Affiliate Transactions (12 U.S.C. 371 c and c1) 12 C.F.R. Part 223	Federal Reserve regulation that implements Sections 23A and 23B of Federal Reserve Act. These related laws restrict covered transactions between a bank and its affiliates and require many affiliate transactions to be on market terms.	7
Reg X	Implements RESPA 12 C.F.R. 1024	Regulation originally by HUD but with CFPB as successor, sets out requirements under RESPA, including disclosure requirements and anti-kickback provisions.	

Banking Term	Reference	Definition	Chapter[1]
Reg Y	Implements the BHCA 12 C.F.R. Part 225	Regulation by Fed that implements the Bank Holding Company Act, including application requirements and the list of activities permitted under section 4(c)(8).	4
Reg DD	Truth in Savings 12 C.F.R. Part 1030	Former Fed regulation transferred to CFPB that implements the Truth in Savings Act. Provides for uniform disclosures to depositors so they can easily compare rates and restrictions regarding savings accounts.	
Repo	Repurchase Agreement	A financial transaction in which a party "purchases" a government security form another party and then resells it the next day (overnight repo) or at a specified term (term repo) for the purchase price plus interest. Often an IDI is the repos seller to a customer and the repos is accomplished through a sweep of funds from the customer's DDA as a means to earn interest on the deposit or provide safety of the funds above the FDIC-insured amount. Repos must be secured on behalf of the purchaser with a priority lien on the government securities as if a secured financing.	
Reserves	12 C.F.R. Part 204	Federal Reserve regulations historically required insured depository institutions to maintain reserves against their transaction accounts (primarily NOW and regular checking accounts). The reserve requirements were subject to annual adjustment by the Federal Reserve. The Federal Reserve no longer establishes reserve requirements by law.	5
RESPA	Real Estate Settlement Procedures Act	Sets out required disclosures for mortgage loans and prohibits illegal steering of loans and kickbacks for home mortgage referrals.	
RFC	Resolution Funding Corporation	Created by FIRREA to provide funding for RTC operations during and after the thrift crisis when FSLIC, the insurer for savings and loan associations, ran out of funds.	

Banking Term	Reference	Definition	Chapter[1]
RFI/C(D)	Federal Reserve BHC Rating System for holding companies under $100 billion	The main components of the RFI rating system are risk management practices (R component) and financial condition (F component) of the consolidated organization, and an assessment of the potential impact (I component) of a holding company's nondepository entities on its subsidiary depository institution(s). A holding company under the RFI rating system is assigned a composite rating (C) based on an evaluation and rating of its managerial and financial condition and an assessment of future potential risk to its subsidiary depository institution(s). A holding company under the RFI rating system is also assigned a depository institution (D) component rating that generally mirrors the primary regulator's assessment of the subsidiary depository institution(s).	8
Riegle-Neal	Riegle-Neal Interstate Banking and Branching Efficiency Act of 1994	Eliminates state barriers to national expansion of banks and BHCs. Allows interstate mergers between banks, subject to concentration limits, state laws, and CRA evaluations.	2
ROA	Return on Assets	A ratio of an institution's net earnings to total assets. Often used a benchmark to indicate how well a bank is earning.	
ROE	1. Return on Equity 2. Report of Exam	1. A ratio of a bank's net earnings to total equity. Often used a benchmark to indicate how well a bank is earning. 2. The report examiners deliver to financial institutions following an examination. The report will include exam findings and the rating assigned to the institution. It must be signed by the directors and is considered the confidential property of the banking agency that examined the institution.	

Banking Term	Reference	Definition	Chapter[1]
RTC	Resolution Trust Corporation	Created by FIRREA; given the responsibility of managing and disposing of the assets of failed institutions. An Oversight Board was created to provide supervisory authority over the policies of the RTC.	
RWA	Risk-Weighted Assets	The denominator of the capital requirements, except for the leverage ratio. Assets are assigned risk-weighting amounts that are then applied to determine total assets. Off-balance sheet exposures are also brought on the balance sheet and risk weighted.	6
S&L	Savings and Loan Association or Savings Association	Refers to a state or federally chartered savings and loan association. A depository institution that historically focused its business on mortgage lending and savings. Now it is regulated by the OCC if it is a federal association and the FDIC and the state if it is state chartered.	1, 2, 3
S&LHC	Savings and Loan Holding Company	A company that owns one or more savings associations. SLHC's were regulated by the OTS until July 21, 2011, and are now regulated by the Federal Reserve.	4
Safety and Soundness (or S & S)		The catchall prudential rules applicable to banks/thrifts to assure the health of our financial system. The federal banking agencies have adopted guidelines that establish operational and managerial standards to promote the safety and soundness of federally insured depository institutions. The guidelines set forth standards for internal controls, information systems, internal audit systems, loan documentation, credit underwriting, interest rate exposure, asset growth, compensation, fees and benefits, and asset quality and earnings.	7, 8

Banking Term	Reference	Definition	Chapter[1]
		In general, the safety and soundness guidelines prescribe the goals to be achieved in each area, and each institution is responsible for establishing its own procedures to achieve those goals. If an institution fails to comply with any of the standards set forth in the guidelines, the institution's primary federal regulator may require the institution to submit a plan for achieving and maintaining compliance. If an institution fails to submit an acceptable compliance plan, or it fails in any material respect to implement a compliance plan that has been accepted by its primary federal regulator, the regulator is required to issue an order directing the institution to cure the deficiency.	
SAIF	Savings Association Insurance Fund	Created by FIRREA; insured the deposits of thrifts but later consolidated with BIF into a single fund (the DIF) administered by the FDIC.	
SAR	Suspicious Activity Report	Report required to be filed where deposits or other activities may, but not necessarily, indicate the violation of law or regulation.	8
SCB	Stress Capital Buffer	In April 2018, the Federal Reserve proposed replacing the Capital Conservation Buffer for those firms that go through the Comprehensive Capital Analysis and Review (CCAR) stress test process with a new "stress capital buffer" consisting of: maximum projected decline (peak-to-trough) in a firm's CET1 ratio during the 9-quarter stress horizon under the "severely adverse" scenario, plus four quarters of the firm's planned common stock dividends.	

Banking Term	Reference	Definition	Chapter[1]
SEC	Securities and Exchange Commission	The SEC is a federal agency created to protect investors and maintain the integrity of the securities markets (exchanges and over-the-counter markets). It has rulemaking authority and enforces the Securities Act of 1933 and the Securities Exchange Act of 1934, as well as the Investment Advisor Act of 1949, the Investment Company Act of 1940, and the Trust Indenture Act.	
SFHA	Standard Flood Hazard Area	The areas for which flood insurance is available under the NFIP as determined by FEMA. Lenders must document the flood hazard determination as part of the mortgage lending process.	
SICC	Standard Industrial Classification Code	A numerical code developed by the Department of Commerce whereby virtually any business activity has a numerical indicator. This code can be found in financial reference manuals and is utilized by the SEC as part of the periodic filings it requires of registered companies. It is also used by several other governmental authorities, including the Federal Trade Commission and the Antitrust Division of the Department of Justice.	
SIDD	Separately Identifiable Department or Division	Has relevance in connection with certain advisory activities under GLBA that banks may either conduct through a subsidiary or through a SIDD.	
SIFI	Systemically Important Financial Institution	FHC or non-bank supervised by the Federal Reserve as deemed systemically important under Dodd-Frank.	4
SLA	Shared Loss Agreement	Used by the FDIC in connection with the resolution of failed institutions to keep assets in the banking sector and minimize losses. Winning bidders for the deposits of failed institutions enter into SLAs with the FDIC.	

Banking Term	Reference	Definition	Chapter[1]
SMDIA	Standard Maximum Deposit Insurance Amount	It is the amount of FDIC insurance on accounts at banks and thrifts. Single accounts (owned by one person with no beneficiaries): $250,000 per owner; Joint Accounts (two or more persons with no beneficiaries): $250,000 per co-owner; IRAs and other certain retirement accounts: $250,000 per owner; Revocable trust accounts: Each owner is insured up to $250,000 for each unique eligible beneficiary named or identified in the revocable trust, subject to specific limitations and requirements.	3
Spence Act	Savings and Loan Holding Company Act of 1959	Created a temporary moratorium on acquisition of additional thrifts by multi-thrift holding companies, and it limited S&L Holding Companies to controlling only a single thrift. Established the regulatory framework for holding companies that owned more than one thrift.	4
SRO	Self-regulatory Organization	A membership-based organization that creates and enforces rules for members based on the federal securities laws. SROs, which are overseen by the SEC, are the front line in regulating broker-dealers.	
Sweep		Refers to a number of financial transactions between a bank and its customers pursuant to which funds above a target balance are moved out of a customer account and then are returned the next morning or at the term. Sweeps allow DDA funds to earn interest and/or provide safety above the FDIC-insured amount. Sweeps can be into repos, money market funds, MMDA's, affiliate banks, etc.	

Banking Term	Reference	Definition	Chapter[1]
TAG	Transaction Account Guarantee	A guarantee of the FDIC that provided customers of participating institutions with full coverage on transaction accounts. It was one of the arsenal of programs put in place to avert the 2008 financial crisis, especially to prevent liquidity crises. Dodd-Frank continued TAG until December 31, 2012, and the CARES act permitted the FDIC to reinstate it until December 31, 2020.	
Tailoring	12 C.F.R Part 252	Under Crapo, the process by which the Federal Reserve determines what holding companies are subject to what types of enhanced prudential regulation. For this purpose, the Federal Reserve identified categories I-IV for holding companies of $100 billion in assets and above, with G-SIBs as Category I.	4
TARP	Troubled Asset Relief Program	Established under EESA and was intended to provide a mechanism for the purchase of troubled assets from financial institutions under either an auction option (if there is a market price) or a direct purchase option and, in the latter situation, may take a non-voting equity interest in the selling institution. It turned into a mechanism to infuse capital into institutions through Treasury's purchases of preferred stock and warrants.	
TBTF	Too Big to Fail	A widely held belief that certain very large financial institutions would cause widespread systemic problems if they were to fail. Title II of DFA is dedicated to mitigation of TBTF.	
Texas Ratio		A leading indicator of financial institutions that may fail—adversely classified assets plus OREO divided by tangible equity capital plus reserves. A Texas ratio of 100% is the sign of a troubled bank.	

Banking Term	Reference	Definition	Chapter[1]
THC	Thrift holding company	See S&LHC.	4
Thrift		A term used generally to apply to S&Ls.	3
Tier 1	Tier 1 Capital Ratio	The core measure of a bank's financial strength from a regulator's point of view. It consists primarily of shareholders' equity but may also include preferred stock that is irredeemable and non-cumulative and retained earnings.	6
Tier 2	Tier 2 Capital	Capital not included in Tier 1, typically subordinated debt, preferred stock that is not perpetual or accumulates skipped dividends, and part of the ALLL. It is used to calculate the Total Risk-based Capital Ratio.	6
TILA	Truth in Lending Act	Initial and subsequent legislation establishing uniform nationwide consumer protection in lending and subsequently leasing of family homes and household items by requiring uniform disclosures of information as to the terms of the loans/leases. Subparts are: FCBA (Fair Credit Billing Act); FCCCPA (Fair Credit and Credit Card Protection Act); HELCPA (Home Equity Lines of Credit Protection Act); and HOPEA (Home Ownership and Equity Protection Act).	
TISA	Truth in Savings Act	Part of the larger Federal Deposit Insurance Corporation Improvement Act of 1991 that is implemented by Reg DD. It established uniformity in the disclosure of terms and conditions regarding interest and fees when giving out information on or opening a new savings account to allow the consumer to make informed decisions.	

Banking Term	Reference	Definition	Chapter[1]
TLAC	Total loss-absorbing capacity	For domestic GSIBs, DFA requires the Federal Reserve to set a minimum level of long-term debt that could be used to recapitalize these firms' critical operations upon failure. The TLAC requirement can be met with both regulatory capital and long-term debt. The debt would convert to equity upon failure so that shareholders, not taxpayers, would absorb the losses.	
Transfer Date		The date under Dodd-Frank on which many of the bank regulatory changes occurred (July 21, 2011).	
Treasury	US Department of the Treasury	Supervises the federal banking system.	
TRID	**T**ruth-in-Lending **R**ESPA **I**ntegrated **D**isclosure	Includes integrated home mortgage disclosures required to be created by the CFPB under Dodd-Frank.	
TRuPs	Trust Preferred Securities	These instruments, which were issued by a special purpose entity (SPE) created by a BHC, qualified under GAAP as minority interests in a consolidated subsidiary and therefore as regulatory capital. In 1996, the Federal Reserve expanded the definition of cumulative preferred stock to TRuPS, which could count as capital within a 25% Tier 1 sublimit. However, under both DFA and Basel III, TRuPS were excluded from capital, except securities that were issued prior to May 19, 2010, by bank holding companies with less than $15 billion of assets as of December 31, 2009, may be retained as Tier I Capital subject to certain restrictions.	
UFIRS	Uniform Financial Institution Rating System	Internal supervisory tool for evaluating the soundness of financial institutions on a uniform basis and for identifying those institutions requiring special attention or concern, adopted by the FFIEC on November 13, 1979.	8

Banking Term	Reference	Definition	Chapter[1]
UIGEA	Unlawful Internet Gambling Enforcement Act of 2006	The law prohibits "any person engaged in the business of betting or wagering from knowingly accepting payments in connection with the participation of another person in unlawful Internet gambling." The Federal Reserve has rulemaking authority.	
Unitary S&LHC	Unitary Thrift/ Savings Association Holding Company	A holding company of only one federal or state savings association that was grandfathered under GLBA and may engage in any activity, including any commercial activity.	4
USA PATRIOT Act	Uniting and Strengthening America by Providing Appropriate Tools Required to Intercept and Obstruct Terrorism Act of 2001	Expands the authority of US law enforcement agencies for the stated purpose of fighting terrorism in the United States and abroad. Among its provisions: increases the ability of law enforcement agencies to search telephone, e-mail communications, medical, financial, and other records; eases restrictions on foreign intelligence gathering within the United States; expands the Secretary of the Treasury's authority to regulate financial transactions, particularly those involving foreign individuals and entities; and enhances the discretion of law enforcement and immigration authorities in detaining and deporting immigrants suspected of terrorism-related acts; also expands the definition of terrorism to include domestic terrorism, thus enlarging the number of activities to which the USA Patriot Act's expanded law enforcement powers can be applied. Title III of the Act is known formally as the International Money Laundering Abatement and Anti-Terrorist Financing Act of 2001 (IMLA Act). Expands the duties of banks in reporting high-risk activities, it also substantially raises the stakes for non-compliance with federal money laundering legislation and increases the scope of businesses now required to participate in anti-money laundering efforts.	

Banking Term	Reference	Definition	Chapter[1]
USPAP	Uniform Standards of Professional Appraisal Practice	Quality control standards applicable for appraisal analysis and reports in the United States and its territories and Canada.	
VaR	Value-at-risk	Banks and BHCs whose trading activity equals 10% or more of its total assets or equals $1 billion or more are subject to holding capital for market risk. They must measure their market risk using a VaR measurement model and, subject to parameters in the market risk rule, hold sufficient levels of Tier 3 capital to cover the exposure.	
Volcker Rule	Section 619 of Dodd-Frank, known colloquially as the "Volcker Rule" because of its patronage by former Federal Reserve Board chairman Paul Volcker	An amendment to the BHC Act that restricts banks from making certain kinds of speculative investments that do not benefit their customers. Specifically, it prohibits insured depository institutions and their affiliates from: (i) engaging in "proprietary trading;" (ii) acquiring or retaining any equity, partnership or other ownership interest in a hedge fund or private equity fund; and (iii) sponsoring a hedge fund or a private equity fund.	4
Well capitalized		Banks/thrifts and their holding companies (except for BHCs with less than $3 billion in assets) must be well capitalized for numerous regulatory purposes. BHCs and all bank/thrift subsidiaries must be well capitalized to be FHCs. The measures under Basel I are: A leverage ratio of Tier 1 Capital to total assets of 5% or greater; a ratio of Tier 1 Capital to total risk-weighted assets of 6% or greater; and a ratio of Total Capital to total risk-weighted assets of 10% or greater.	4, 6

Banking Term	Reference	Definition	Chapter[1]
Well managed		Banks/thrifts and their holding companies must be well managed for numerous regulatory purposes. BHCs and all bank/thrift subsidiaries must be well capitalized to be FHCs. It means that the Management rating in the CAMELS ratings was a 1 or 2.	4, 8
Wild card		A law that matches powers of one type of financial institution to another. Usually, a state law that permits a state bank to engage in the activities permissible to a national bank by interpretation of the OCC. However, it may work the other way as well.	3

About the Author and Editor

Karol K. Sparks is a partner in the Financial Institutions Group of Barack Ferrazzano, LLP, Chicago, Illinois. Her practice concentrates on corporate activities and regulatory issues of financial institutions, about which she has counseled banks for over 40 years.

A past chair of the Banking Law Committee of the Business Law Section of the American Bar Association (1998–2002), she has been an active member of the committee since 1985. She was an elected member of the Council of the Business Law Section of the ABA, the governing body of that organization, for a term ending in August 2008. She chaired the Publications Board of the Business Law Section of the ABA for a term ending in August 2014.

Karol is the author of *Keys to Banking Law*, published by the American Bar Association, now in its third edition, and of the legal treatise *Insurance Activities of Banks* (first edition published by Aspen Law & Business in 1998; second edition in 2012), which is updated annually. She is a frequent lecturer and educator on issues relating to the regulation of financial institutions. From 2009 until 2013, she was an adjunct professor at Wake Forest University School of Law, having previously taught at the University of Iowa College of Law as an adjunct from 2001–2007. Starting in January of 2014, she joined the Graduate Program in Banking and Financial Law of the Boston University School of Law as a lecturer in law in the LL.M program, from which she retired in 2017. She is a member of the founding faculty of Banking Law Basics, an ABA-CLE course offered in June and October of each year from 1998–2011, and its successor course, Fundamentals of Banking Law, sponsored by the Boston University School of Law and, beginning in 2021, by the Chicago-Kent College of Law in Chicago.

John M. Geiringer is a chapter co-author and the editor of *Banking Law Essentials*. John is a partner in Barack Ferrazzano, Chicago, Illinois. As the Regulatory Section Leader of the Firm's Financial Institutions Group, John concentrates his practice on regulatory, governance, and investigative matters involving financial institutions.

He is a frequent speaker and author in the financial institutions area on issues surrounding banking regulations, examinations, and enforcement actions. He is on the faculty of Fundamentals of Banking Law and teaches banking law and regulation at Chicago-Kent College of Law's Graduate

Program in Financial Services Law and serves on the board of advisors of its Institute for Compliance. He is the co-editor of the two-volume edition, *Advising Illinois Financial Institutions*, in which he wrote a chapter on bank enforcement issues. John is a former vice-chair of the American Bar Association's Banking Law Committee.

John also devotes significant time to Bank Secrecy Act and anti-money laundering issues. He is on the advisory board of the Anti-Money Laundering Association and is the president of its Midwest Chapter. He has frequently lectured on the subject, including at Georgetown University's Center for Security Studies, Boston University School of Law, and Chicago-Kent College of Law, where he serves as a co-director of its Center for National Security and Human Rights Law. He is the editor and author of a chapter in the upcoming book, *Countering the Financing of Terrorism: Law and Policy*, and is a Certified Anti-Money Laundering Specialist (CAMS).

Prior to joining Barack Ferrazzano in 1999, John was both a bank regulator and a compliance consultant. He served as legal counsel for the Illinois bank regulatory agency. John also obtained practical experience with respect to bank operations and compliance issues as a regulatory consultant with a regional accounting firm, performing compliance reviews and training for a variety of financial institutions.

About the Contributors

J. Brent McCauley contributed to the information in Chapter 4 on financial holding companies. He is a partner in the Barack Ferrazzano Financial Institutions Group. Brent has over 30 years of experience in the financial services industry. He began his career as an examiner with the Office of Thrift Supervision in 1989, where he also worked as a fraud investigator. After law school, Brent was senior counsel in the legal department of the Federal Reserve Bank of Chicago, handling complex regulatory and supervisory matters. He currently represents all types of financial institutions including securities broker-dealers, insurance companies, investment advisers as well as banks, thrifts and their holding companies in mergers and acquisitions/corporate and regulatory matters.

Stanley F. Orszula updated and edited the Second and Third Editions of Chapter 11 of Keys to Banking Law, Examination and Enforcement, which contributed to Chapter 8 of Banking Law Essentials. He is a partner in the Barack Ferrazzano Financial Institutions Group with extensive experience providing strategic counsel to banks on compliance and regulatory issues, fintech, banking-as-a-service (BaaS), general banking corporate matters, secured lending, government lending programs, distressed loans and assets, failed bank receiverships and note sales. Stan's background includes experience serving as a Lieutenant in the United States Navy Judge Advocate Corps, counsel with the FDIC, sitting on the board of a financial institution, and representing banks in private practice for almost 20 years. Stan frequently speaks and writes about fintech and BasS developments affecting banks.

Andrea Sill originally authored the discussion of Regulation O in Chapter 6 of Keys to Banking Law, portions of which are included in Chapter 7 of Banking Law Essentials. Andrea is a partner of in the Barack Ferrazzano Financial Institutions Group and concentrates her practice on bank regulatory and corporate matters. She has extensive experience working on a variety of regulatory and corporate matters, including mergers and acquisitions, equity and debt offerings, regulatory applications, corporate governance, compliance and enforcement matters. Prior to joining the Firm, Andrea served as legal counsel to the banking division of the Illinois Office of Banks and Real Estate, now known as the Illinois Department of Financial and Professional Regulation.

About the Contributors